# A NEW COMMANDMENT

# SHEILA KIRWAN
# LINDA P. GARLAND

# A NEW COMMANDMENT

And now I give you a new commandment: love one another.
As I have loved you, so you must love one another.
(John 13:34)

## The Light of the World Series 1

Gill and Macmillan

Published in Ireland by
Gill and Macmillan Ltd
Goldenbridge
Dublin 8
with associated companies throughout the world

© Linda P. Garland and Sheila Kirwan, 1989, 1991
© Artwork, Gill and Macmillan Ltd, 1989, 1991
0 7171 1897 5

Print origination by
Seton Music Graphics Ltd, Bantry, Co Cork,
Design and illustrations by
Design Image, Dublin
Original cover design by
Paul Francis

Nihil obstat
Oliver V. Brennan B.D., M.A.
Imprimatur
✠ Tomás Cardinal Ó Fiaich, Archbishop of Armagh

# CONTENTS

# ACKNOWLEDGMENTS

The authors wish to thank the following for their helpful assistance during the pre-paration of this book: Anne Kenna, Fr Bill Reilly, Fr Oliver Brennan, School Catechists who reviewed drafts of the text, staff of Gill and Macmillan, Publishers.

Unless otherwise stated, all Scripture quotations are from the Good News Bible, published by The Bible Societies and Collins, Old Testament © American Bible Society 1976, New Testament (Good News for Modern Man), © American Bible Society 1964, 1971, 1976. Reproduced by permission.

The quotation from the Book of Sirach is from the Revised Standard Version of the Bible published by the Catholic Truth Society, © National Council of the Churches of Christ, New York.

'The Trial of the Scillitan Christians' is reproduced from *Harlequinade* by Janet Green (Church House Publishing: 1982) by permission of the Central Board of Finance of the Church of England.

# PHOTO CREDITS

For permission to reproduce photographs, grateful acknowledgment is made to the following:

Stephen O'Reilly: pages 5 (both), 7 (three), 29, 38, 66, 90, 91, 94 (top), 99 (bottom), 132 (all except sheep sale), 133 (both), 155, 157;
Barnaby's Picture Library: pages 7 (netball), 95, 132 (sheep sale);
Sally and Richard Greenhill: pages 7 (top right), 50, 94 (bottom), 96, 150;
Sonia Halliday: pages 57 (all except synagogue), 60, 61, 76, 98, 141, 143 (top), 145;
Zefa: pages 57 (synagogue), 58 (both), 146;
Robert Allen: pages 94 (middle), 99 (top), 101, 105, 113, 136, 142, 143 (middle and bottom), 160;
Bridgeman Art Library: pages 111 (top), 147;
Office of Public Works: page 111 (bottom);
Corrymeela Community: page 112;
Ancient Art and Architecture Collection: page 125;
Spectrum Colour Library: page 139;
SIPA Press: page 151.

For their kind co-operation, thanks are due to Fintan Gavin, Holy Cross College, Clonliffe and Balbriggan Community College.
*Photo Research:* Anne-Marie Ehrlich.

# UNIT I

# INTRODUCTION

## ME

## CHAPTER 1

▼

**The Golden Eagle**

A man found an eagle's egg and placed it under a brooding hen. The eaglet hatched with the chickens and grew to be like them. He clucked and cackled; scratched the earth for worms; flapped his wings and managed to fly a few feet in the air.

Years passed. One day, the eagle, now grown old, saw a magnificent bird above him in the sky. It glided in graceful majesty against the powerful wind, with scarcely a movement of its golden wings.

Spellbound, the eagle asked, 'Who's that?'

'That's the King of the Birds, the eagle,' said his neighbour. 'He belongs to the sky. We belong to earth — we're chickens.'

So the eagle lived and died a chicken for that's what he thought he was.

(*The Song of the Bird* by Anthony de Mello, S.J.)

## QUESTIONS

1. What made the eagle think he was a chicken?
2. Why did the eagle not realise that he could fly?
3. Can you imagine what might have happened if somebody had told the eagle that he could fly if he tried?
4. The eagle never discovered his great talent for flying. Do you feel that people can have talents and not discover them? Explain your answer.

Every one of us is capable of being great in some way. God has made each person unique, and everyone has special gifts. God has given most people some obvious gifts. But people also have hidden talents, which, like the eagle, they may never discover. The more we learn about ourselves, the more we will discover and use our special gifts.

1 Corinthians 12:4–11

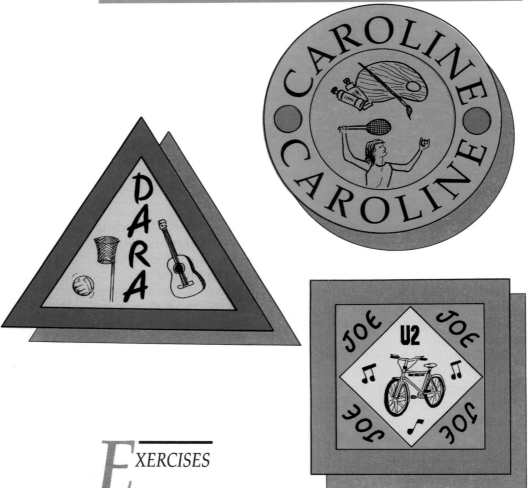

# EXERCISES

1. Finish these sentences:
   (a) I like . . .
   (b) I don't like . . .
   (c) My favourite people are . . .
   (d) One day I hope to . . .
2. Is there anything you enjoy doing now which you were not able to do when you were seven years old?

# GROUP WORK

Divide into small groups of four or five people. Tell each other the answers you gave to the above questions.

# SOME MORE EXERCISES

1. What abilities or talents do you share with the rest of the people in your class? (e.g. listening, smiling)
2. Do you have any special interest or hobby which is not shared by everyone in the class?

During the coming year you will have many opportunities to learn more about yourself: in class, with your friends and at home. Remember, being a great person doesn't mean having exactly the same gifts as everyone else. Being great means *finding* and *using* your own special gifts, which you have received from God.

*Reflection*: 'You created every part of me; you put me together in my mother's womb. I praise you because you are to be feared; all you do is strange and wonderful. I know it with all my heart. When my bones were being formed, carefully put together in my mother's womb, when I was growing there in secret, you knew that I was there.' Psalm 139:13–15

*Action*: Make your own personal name badge, using cardboard and a pin. Decorate it to show your talents.

*Song*: 'I Have Called You By Your Name'

*Prayer*: Lord, thank you for creating me as I am. Help me to learn more about myself during the coming year. Amen.

# OUR CLASS

## CHAPTER 2
▼

What do each of these cartoons have in common?

Do you have plans for this year? Maybe there is something you want to do, or something you would like to succeed at. This is called having an aim. You will probably have to work hard to achieve your aims, like the people in the cartoons.

# *E*XERCISES

1. What are your aims for this year? Describe them using these headings:
   (a) at school
   (b) at home
   (c) other aims.
2. What will you have to do to achieve those aims?

# *G*ROUP WORK

1. Does your group share any common aims?
2. How could you help each other to achieve those aims?
3. Report your findings to the whole class.

# *Q*UESTIONS

1. What are the aims that the whole class has?
2. How could you work together to achieve them?

If your class has an aim and you are working hard together to achieve that aim, then you could become a *community*.

In a community people care about one another and try to help each other. Working alone to achieve an aim can be lonely. Our hopes and dreams can seem impossible if no one else believes in them. When we are part of a community, other people encourage us to keep trying, and we also help them. Living and working as a community can be fun, especially when we celebrate together, on birthdays, or at Christmas, or whenever we achieve an aim.

# SOME MORE EXERCISES

1.  This year you have the chance to build a new community together. There are many ways of making a community strong—*trust, friendship, teamwork, thanks.*
    Give examples to show how each of these could make the life of this class community better.
2.  Add some of your own examples to this list.
3.  Give some examples to show what could harm the community, or cause problems in the class.
4.  Draw a plan of
    (a) your classroom
    (b) your school.
5.  Make a drawing of your school crest.

*Reflection*: 'Your life in Christ makes you strong, and his love comforts you. You have fellowship with the Spirit, and you have kindness and compassion for one another. I urge you, then, to make me completely happy by having the same thoughts, sharing the same love, and being one in soul and mind. Don't do anything from selfish ambition or from a cheap desire to boast, but be humble towards one another, always considering others better than yourselves. And look out for one another's interests, not just for your own.' Philippians 2:1–4

*Action*: Working in small groups, compose a short prayer. Pool all the most interesting ideas, and write the prayer on a wall poster. Ask the teachers in the school to use it with your class instead of other prayers.

*Song*: 'This is My Will'

*Prayer*: Thank you Father for our class community. Teach us how to get on well together. Amen.

# COMMUNITY IS GOOD

## CHAPTER 3
▼

# GROUP WORK

1. All of these people need communities in different ways. Divide into five groups. In each group make up a story to show how one of the people above needs a community.
2. Explain how his/her community needs the person you wrote about in your group.
3. Share your story with the rest of the class.

It is good to be part of a community. Ask any football player or Girl Guide — each of them needs others in order to be really good at what they do.

No one likes to be left out, to feel unwanted. When we work together as a team, in a community, we know that we are really needed, and this makes us feel good about ourselves. As we learn to trust others and share our time, our ideas and our feelings with them, our friendships grow stronger and we become happier.

> From the very beginning God our Father wanted us to be happy together in communities. 'It is not good for a person to be completely alone,' He said. That is why He gives us families, friends and neighbours — so that we can all feel wanted and loved, and can learn to love others.

# *Q*UESTIONS

1. As a class try to think of as many different communities as you can. List them on the blackboard.
2. What do you like about being part of your class community?

# *E*XERCISES

1. Do you need your class community in any way? Explain.
2. Most people belong to different communities. Mention some communities to which you belong. Briefly describe them. For example:
   (a) I belong to a family.
   (b) Our aim is . . .
   (c) We work hard together by . . .
   (d) I like this community because . . .
   (e) I need this community because . . .
   (f) We could improve our community by . . .
3. Write a short account of the parish to which you belong.

*Reflection*: '. . . agree, all of you, in what you say, so that there will be no divisions among you. Be completely united . . .'
1 Corinthians 1:10b

*Action*:  Think of an action which you can do this week to show that you want your class to be a loving community.

*Song*:  'Glory and Praise to our God'

*Prayer*:  Our Father, thank you for the communities we live in. Help us to make them better every day.  Amen.

# OUR RELIGION CLASS

## CHAPTER 4

▼

**Race Against the Clock!**

Read the guidelines carefully. You will need dice to play this game.

*Guidelines for Playing*

1. Throw a six to start.
2. Obey all instructions in the square you land on.
3. You cannot remain on a green square. If you land on a green square, you must go back one square. If you land on a blue square go back to Start.
4. If you throw a 1, 2, 3, 4, or 5 go directly to Finish.
5. The person who first reaches Finish wins.

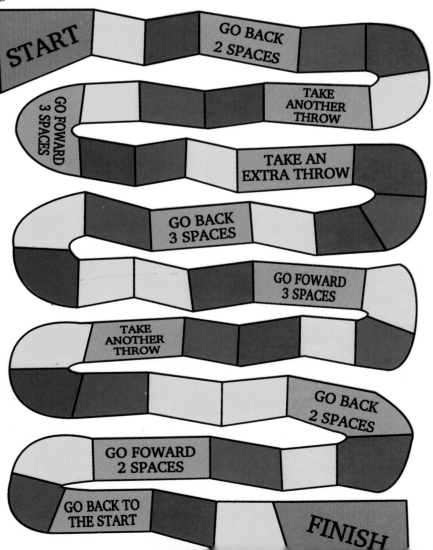

START

GO BACK 2 SPACES

GO FOWARD 3 SPACES

TAKE ANOTHER THROW

TAKE AN EXTRA THROW

GO BACK 3 SPACES

GO FOWARD 3 SPACES

TAKE ANOTHER THROW

GO BACK 2 SPACES

GO FOWARD 2 SPACES

GO BACK TO THE START

FINISH

If you followed the guidelines for the game, you should have reached the Finish in a few minutes. Perhaps you were too busy to read them and so you lost the race.

# QUESTIONS

1. Are there other situations in which it is very important to follow the guidelines? Explain.
2. What would happen in those situations if you did not follow the guidelines?

God says, 'I have called you by your name, you are mine.' Because we belong to God, who created us, we are very special. God wants us to be happy, loving people. In our religion class we will learn more about God's plan for us, and how we can follow this plan. Our lives are much more important than a game, so as well as giving us some guidelines to follow, God is always with us to guide and help us whenever we ask Him. We know that God wants us to love each other, and be ready to forgive one another. But it can be difficult to love or be nice to someone who has hurt us. This is when we need to ask God to help us. We find God's guidelines in Scripture and in the teaching of the Church. Our parents, teachers and others also explain God's plan to us. In the religion class we can learn more about God's guidelines and we can also put them into practice in our daily lives.

# EXERCISES

1. What have you already learned about God's plans for you?
2. Where did you learn this?
3. What would you most like to learn this year in religion class?
4. Why is it important to ask God for His guidance? Explain your answer.
5. Are there any similarities or differences between the guidelines for a game and God's guidelines for your life?

*Reflection*: 'Jesus said, "I am the way, the truth, and the life; no one goes to the Father except by me."' John 14:6

*Action*: Design a poster to display in the school hall, which shows one of God's guidelines for a happy life.

*Song*: 'Seek Ye First'

*Prayer*: Lord, help me to know and follow your plan for me each day. Amen.

# UNIT II

## LOVE / REFUSING TO LOVE

## LOVE IS . . .

### CHAPTER 5

In 1941, the Second World War was taking place in Europe. At first it seemed as if the Germans were winning; but the tide turned in Russia in 1941 when the Germans had to surrender:

'In 1941, Mama took me back to Moscow. There I saw our enemy for the first time. If my memory is right, nearly 20,000 German war prisoners were to be marched in a single column through the streets of Moscow.

The pavements swarmed with onlookers, cordoned off by soldiers and police. The crowd was mostly women. Russian women with hands roughened by hard work, lips untouched by lipstick and thin, hunched shoulders which had borne half the burden of the war. Every one of them must have had a father or husband or brother or son killed by the Germans.

They gazed with hatred in the direction from which the column was to appear. At last we saw it.

The generals marched at the head, massive chins stuck out, lips folded disdainfully, their whole demeanour meant to show superiority over their plebeian victors . . .

The women were clenching their fists. The soldiers and policemen had all they could do to hold them back.

All at once something happened to them.

They saw German soldiers, thin, unshaven, wearing dirty, bloodstained bandages, hobbling on crutches or leaning on the shoulders of their comrades; the soldiers walked with their heads down.

The street became dead silent — the only sound was the shuffling of boots and the thumping of crutches. Then I saw an elderly woman in broken down boots push herself forward and touch a policeman's shoulder, saying: 'Let me through.' There must have been something about her that made him step aside.

She went up to the column, took from inside her coat something wrapped in a coloured handkerchief and unfolded it. It was a crust of black bread. She pushed it awkwardly into the pocket of a soldier, so exhausted that he was tottering on his feet. And now suddenly from every side women were running towards the soldiers, pushing into their hands bread, cigarettes, whatever they had.

The soldiers were no longer enemies. They were People.'

(Yevtushenko, from *Quotes and Anecdotes for Preachers and Teachers*, compiled by Anthony P. Castle)

# QUESTIONS

1. How did the Russians feel about the German soldiers at the beginning of the story? Why?
2. How do you think the Germans felt at the beginning of the story? Why?
3. Did the Russian people or the German soldiers feel differently at the end of the story? Explain.
4. What, in your opinion, is the most important moment in the story? Explain.

# EXERCISES

1. This story has many different messages or meanings. What is the most important meaning or message for you?
2. Write a story of your own which has similar messages or meanings.

> Love means putting the other person first. It means thinking about what others need and want, and trying to treat them as we ourselves would like to be treated. When people have hurt us, we can love them by being forgiving. If people are hungry, we can show love by giving them food. We have to make an effort to really love someone. Parents who seldom go out so that they can buy school books and uniforms are showing how much they love their children. In the same way a teenager who misses a favourite TV programme in order to help get the dinner, or do the shopping, is doing something loving.

3. In the story, how did the old woman show love for the soldiers?
4. Was it easy for her to do this? Explain.
5. Write down the names of three people who love you (for example, parent, friend, relation). How do they show that they love you?

*Reflection*: 'Love is patient and kind; it is not jealous or conceited or proud; love is not ill-mannered or selfish or irritable; love does not keep a record of wrongs; love is not happy with evil, but is happy with the truth. Love never gives up; and its faith, hope and patience never fail.' 1 Corinthians 13:4–7

*Action*: Think of a way to show your love for someone in your home, and put it into action.

*Song*: 'The Love Round'

*Prayer*: Lord, thank you for all the people who love me and show me they care. Amen.

# GOD LOVES ALL PEOPLE

## CHAPTER 6
▼

In the beginning there was absolutely nothing.

Then God created the heavens and the earth.
God said, 'Let there be light,' and there it was.

He called the light 'day' and the darkness 'night'.

It was wonderful!

God surrounded the earth with life-giving air.

God said, 'Let the dry land appear.'

The waters that were gathered together He called 'seas'.

It was marvellous!

Then God thought of oaks, daffodils, blackberry bushes and strawberries.

It was stupendous!

Then God created the sun, the moon and all the stars.

And there were seasons and years.

God said, 'Let there be swarms of living creatures in the waters and in the sky: flying birds, great sea monsters and little fishes.

It was tremendous!

'And let the dry land bring forth creatures of every kind,' He said.

By now the earth was full of the most fantastic creatures! And then God decided to create people.

It was the Supreme Moment of creation.

Because people were different.

They could laugh, love, think, choose and invent.

God put them in charge of His creation. He said, 'They're like me,' and He loved them.

And then God rested.

# $Q$ UESTIONS

1.  How does this Bible story make you feel?
2.  Who is the main character in the story?
3.  What is this character like?
4.  What does this character do in the story?
5.  What is the difference between people and all the other things God created?
6.  Does anything change between the beginning and end of the story? Why do these changes happen?
7.  What is the most important moment in the story? Why?
8.  Why do you think God bothered creating all these things?

# $E$ XERCISES

1.  What does this story tell us about:
    (a) God
    (b) the universe
    (c) ourselves?
2.  What meaning or message do you find in this story?
3.  Could this story have any influence on the way we think or behave?

The story of creation does not tell us in detail how or when God made the world, but it does show that God has loved people from the very beginning. He shows this love by giving us life and by giving us the power to love each other. The world is full of signs that God loves us: the plants provide food, clothing and shelter; the sun gives heat and light; streams and lakes provide water. Because He loves us, God has also given us the ability to use these gifts wisely, so that everyone can benefit from them.

*Reflection*: 'Then God said, "And now we will make human beings; they will be like us and resemble us. They will have power over the fish, the birds and all the animals, domestic and wild, large and small." So God created human beings, making them to be like Himself. He created them male and female.' Genesis 1:26–27

*Action*: Make up a play or mime showing the creation of the world.

*Song*: 'Mighty Lord'

*Prayer*: Dear God, we praise you because you are so loving, powerful and good. Thank you for giving us so many wonderful people and beautiful things. Amen.

# GOD LOVES ME

**CHAPTER 7 ▶**

God tells each one of us in so many ways that He really loves us. On this page you can see some of the gifts which God gives us to show that He loves us.

# EXERCISES

1. Look at the picture on the previous page. Choose the things in it which you like best. Explain how they show you that God loves you.

In order to show us how much He loved us, God sent His Son, Jesus, to live among us and show us God's love in a special way. Because Jesus is the Son of God, everything he did and said shows us what God is like. By healing the sick, Jesus showed that God loves the sick and wants to help them. By the power of God's love, sick people may be cured or may be given the strength to bear their illness. By forgiving people's sins, Jesus showed that God loves people even when they have done wrong. This means that if *we* are sick, or in any kind of trouble, God still loves us and wants to help us.

2. Read about an incident in Jesus' life on earth: Jesus and the little children — Mark 10:13–16 (your teacher will help you to find it in your Bible).
   (a) Why do you think the people wanted Jesus to touch their children?
   (b) What was the attitude of the disciples towards the children?
   (c) What was Jesus' attitude towards the children?
   (d) In your opinion, what is Jesus' attitude to young people?
   (e) How does God show His love for you as a young person
      (i) through other people
      (ii) through nature?

*Reflection*: 'See how much the Father has loved us! His love is so great that we are called God's children — and so, in fact, we are.' 1 John 3:1

*Action*: Do a class project called 'God loves Us'. Work in groups, each group preparing drawings, pictures, collages, stories etc., on some aspect of God's love for your class. For example, one group might choose nature, another hobbies, or families. Put all the work on a wall in your classroom under one project heading.

*Song*: 'Sing to the Mountains'

*Prayer*: Lord, thank you for loving us and for showing your love in so many ways. We thank you especially for sending us Jesus, your Son, who shows us your love in a special way. Amen.

# LOVING GOD AND OTHERS

## CHAPTER 8
▼

### A Circle of Friendship

Draw a circle of friendship; write in the names of all your favourite people.

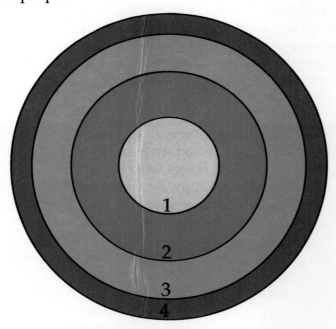

1.  Draw this design in your copy.
2.  In circle 1 fill in the first names of the people you know and love best.
3.  In circle 2 fill in the first names of the people with whom you are friendly.
4.  Fill in circle 3 with the names or a description of people that you don't know very well but perhaps see quite often, for example, the shop assistant.
5.  You may meet some people once or twice and never see them again. Write a description of some of these people into circle 4, for example, an American tourist, a basketball team.

Because God loves us, He gave us the ability to love God and other people. One way in which we show our love for God is by loving others. We show our love for different people in different ways.

# QUESTIONS

1. How do you show your love for the people you love best?
2. For your friends?
3. For the people in your other circles?
4. Into which circle would you put yourself?
5. How do you show your love for yourself?
6. Where would you put God in the circle of friendship?
7. Can you think of any ways in which you could show God that you love Him?

Jesus said: 'I want to give you a new commandment: love each other.' Jesus asks us to love each other because this is God's plan for us. God wants us to be happy people, and we can only be really happy by loving each other. Every time we love ourselves or someone else, we are doing what God wants. We are also behaving a little bit like God does. God gives us gifts to show that He loves us.

We too can give presents to people to show that we care. If someone tells us they are sorry for treating us badly, we can forgive them, just as God forgives us. Whenever we help other people in any way we are treating them the way God treats us — with love and concern.

# EXERCISES

1. How are you behaving like God when you love someone?
2. In what way are your loving actions different to God's loving actions?

*Reflection*: 'And now I give you a new commandment: love one another. As I have loved you, so you must love one another.' John 13:34

*Action*: Make a 'circle of friendship' poster using photographs of yourself, your friends or your family members.

*Song*: 'Make Me a Channel of Your Peace'

*Prayer*: Dear God, thank you for making me able to love myself, others and you. Help me to show my love each day. Amen.

# MAKING CHOICES

## CHAPTER 9

1. Your friend has not studied for his maths test. Should you let him:
   (a) copy all your answers?
   (b) do his best on his own?
   (c) copy some of your answers?

2. Mary has no money to go out on Friday night. Jane always has lots of money and has a habit of leaving it in her coat pocket. Should Mary:
   (a) stay at home on Friday?
   (b) go to see a friend on Friday?
   (c) take £2 that won't be missed?

3. You have just got a new bicycle. Your friend wants to go on a sponsored cycle. You are going away that day. Should you:
   (a) tell him he can't have it?
   (b) say he can have it provided he pays for any damages?
   (c) hand it over immediately — no questions asked?

# EXERCISES

Think about these three situations and the possible solutions.
1. What would be the result of each of the solutions?
2. Which of the solutions are loving solutions and which are unloving?
3. Are the results of the loving solutions similar?
4. Are the results of the unloving solutions similar?
5. Choose the best action in each situation and explain why you think it is the best.

# GROUP WORK

Form small groups and compare your answers to each question in turn. As a group, decide on one answer to each question, and report back to the class.

You will often find *you have a choice between doing something loving and something unloving.* An unloving action may seem easier at the time. For example, if we have to make an effort in order to help someone, it can seem easier not to bother. A runner who seldom trains and who often eats junk food is also taking the easy way out. Things get tough, however, when he tries to race and finds himself a loser. If we are always doing the lazy, mean or unloving thing, we become lazy, mean and unloving people.

The opposite is also true. The more we try to do kind, caring and helpful actions, the nicer and more loving we become. Being a loving person takes a lot of effort, but it makes us better, happier people. For example, if you help a friend with some homework and miss a favourite television programme, you know you are a really worthwhile friend and you can feel proud of yourself.

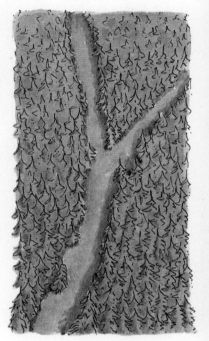

*We often have a choice . . .*

# EXERCISES

1. Give some examples to show when you have a choice between a loving action and an unloving action.
2. Explain the results of both types of actions.
3. Taking one of your own examples, can you say why you might sometimes be tempted to do the unloving thing?

God wants us to be happy always. He knows that if we are always loving, we will be happier people. God allows us to make up our own minds to do the loving or the unloving action.

4. What have you learned about love from this chapter?
5. What have you learned about yourself?

*Reflection*: 'Do not spread lies about anyone, and when some-one is on trial for his life, speak out if your testimony can help him. I am the Lord. Do not bear a grudge against anyone, but settle your differences with him, so that you will not commit a sin because of him.' Leviticus 19:16–17

*Action*: If there is any occasion when you tend to encourage others to do something unloving, rather than something loving, make up your mind to stop.

*Song*: 'Only in God'

*Prayer*: Lord, help us always to choose what is loving and good, and to help others to do the same. Amen.

# REFUSING TO LOVE

## CHAPTER 10

▼

1.

2. Tom and Joe have been friendly for years. Since they went to the post-primary school, Tom has become very friendly with the boys on the football team. Joe is not interested in football. One day at break, a group of footballers starts sneering at Joe, calling him a cissy. Joe is very upset, and looks to Tom to back him up. Tom knows that he will lose his new friends if he stands up for Joe. So he walks off.

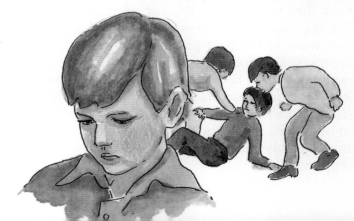

3. Jennifer leaves the house at 10.45 a.m. one Sunday morning to go to Mass. She has always enjoyed the 11.00 a.m. Folk Mass. At the church door she meets her friend Mary:

*Mary:* Hi, Jennifer. Are you going in?

*Jennifer:* Oh, hello Mary. Yes, I'm just on time.

*Mary* (producing a packet of sweets): Don't bother going in today. No one will see us over here in this corner.

*Jennifer:* I don't know, Mary. I'd rather go in.

*Mary:* Why? Your mother will never know, and if anyone asks, you can always say you were feeling sick.

*Jennifer:* It would be great to sit out here and chat. After all, it's only the same thing week after week. (*Thinks — why did I say that? After all, what's forty minutes out of my life, when I think of what God has done for me . . .*)

*Mary:* Well, do what you like, but I'm not going in.

*Jennifer:* Oh, all right. I'll skip it just this once.

*Mary:* Just this once? I haven't gone for months.

Jennifer remembered an old saying: 'The first time you do something wrong is the hardest. It can easily become a habit.'

Carefully examine these three situations. They have something in common. The following questions will help you discover what it is.

1. What has happened to the countryside in the picture? Who has done this? Why? Do you think they realised the harm they were doing? Who or what has been harmed?
2. Did the friendship between Tom and Joe change when they went to the post-primary school? Why did the footballers pick on Joe? What did Tom do? Why? What did Joe feel about this? Did Tom realise that Joe would feel like this? Who or what was harmed in this situation?
3. What happened as a result of Jennifer meeting Mary? Did Jennifer feel right about what she was doing? Was she forced to stay outside? Who or what was harmed by what happened?

30

When we deliberately decide not to love other people, or God, or God's world, we sin. As a result of our sin, we harm ourselves and others, and we also harm our relationship with ourselves, others and God.

# EXERCISES

1. Give an example to show how someone of your age could be unloving to or sin against:
   (a) a friend
   (b) a member of the family
   (c) a tree
   (d) God.
2. In each of your examples, show who or what is harmed by the sin.
3. In each of your examples, explain how relationships could be damaged by the unloving action.

*Reflection*: 'If we say that we have no sin we deceive ourselves . . . But, if we confess our sins to God, we can trust Him . . . He will forgive us our sins . . .' 1 John 1:8–9

*Action*: When you next celebrate the Sacrament of Reconciliation, examine your conscience by asking yourself:

1. Have I been unloving at home? Towards my parents, brothers or sisters?
2. Have I been unloving at school? Towards other students, teachers or other staff?
3. Have I been unloving towards the world I live in? Have I vandalised property? Or been cruel to animals? Or harmed trees or other plants?
4. Have I been unloving towards God? By my actions? By not doing something?

*Song*: 'Turn to Me'

*Prayer*: Lord, help me not to sin, but to be loving towards the world, other people and you. Amen.

# FORGIVENESS

## CHAPTER 11

**Joseph MacMonacle's Diary**
**VERY PRIVATE**

*JULY: Friday, 7.00 p.m.*

I have decided to keep a diary. Maybe it will be published some day and I'll be famous. Nothing much happened today. I watched television this morning until Mam turned it off.

'The holidays won't last for ever,' she said. 'Why don't you go out and play in the sunshine?'

Play! You'd think I was just a kid. A few of the lads were out, so we played a bit of football on the road. Mr Ryan told us not to break any windows and to be careful of the cars. We had no problem with the cars. We apologised to him for cracking his side window. It was only one small pane of glass, but he could have made trouble. He said it was all right and to be more careful in future.

*Saturday, 5.00 p.m.*

My Dad wants to know why we can't go to the park to play football. The park is *miles* away. Well, it takes at least ten minutes to get there. Besides, it's better playing on the road. Mr Ryan's gate posts make great goals. It's a pity his sitting-room window is just behind them. Bobby is a rotten goalie, but I admit it was mostly my fault the window got smashed. Mr Ryan was very decent about it, and said I could pay it off by the week. Nothing much happened in the afternoon.

*Monday, 1.30 p.m.*

I'll probably be writing this diary in prison tomorrow. Today I broke Mr Ryan's new window. This time I wasn't even playing football. I was practising my tennis shots instead. The Ryans' wall is the only one high enough to be of any use. It wasn't quite high enough, however.

'Now that was a stupid thing to do,' said my Dad. He's just great at stating the obvious.

'What did Mr Ryan say to you?' he asked.

I said nothing.

'Do you mean you haven't owned up?'

'Not yet,' I mumbled.

'I suppose you were waiting until you'd broken a few more,' said Dad in a nasty voice. I hate sarcasm.

### Monday, 2.00 p.m.

I can hardly believe it. While I was writing in my diary just now, the doorbell rang, and it was Mr Ryan. I couldn't look at him when my Dad left us together in our sitting-room.

'Have you something to say to me, Joseph?' he asked.

I took a deep breath. 'Mr Ryan, I'm really sorry about breaking the window. It was careless and stupid of me. I knew I was being stupid even before it broke. I suppose you won't believe me.'

'I believe you,' he said quietly.

I looked hopefully at him. 'I'll pay for a new window,' I said.

'But you won't have a penny left for yourself at this rate.'

'I've decided to go with the lads to the park from now on,' I told him.

'That's good,' he said. 'Much safer. I'm glad we had this chat.' Then he left.

There was no big scene, no giving out. My Dad said I was lucky — anyone else would have called the police.

It's much better playing football in the park anyway. It's good fun getting the ball down from the top of the bandstand. Some of the lads want to keep on playing on the road, but Mr Ryan has been so decent, I'm not going to join them.

# QUESTIONS

1. What kind of a person is Joseph?
2. What is Mr Ryan like?
3. Do you think Joseph was sorry for breaking the windows?
4. Are you surprised by Mr Ryan's reaction? Why?
5. How did Mr Ryan's reaction influence Joseph?
6. How do you think Joseph would have felt if Mr Ryan had not forgiven him?

### The Israelites

Once, many years ago, a whole nation of people called the Israelites were kept as slaves by the Egyptians. They were very unhappy: 'And they cried out and God heard their cry.' With many miracles and signs, God helped them to escape into the desert and promised to give them their own country in which to live.

God said: 'I have come down to deliver them out of the land of the Egyptians and to bring them up out of that land to a good and broad land, a land flowing with milk and honey.'

But the new country was a long way off, and the Israelites had to go through many hardships to get there. They began to grumble among themselves. They said they were tired, hungry and thirsty and they wished they were back in Egypt.

'You have brought us out into this wilderness to kill us all with hunger,' they said. They turned against God who had saved them. Eventually however they realised that they needed God. So they asked God to forgive them. God had never stopped loving and caring for them and so He forgave them for their sins against Him. When the people reached the promised land, they tried to love God and follow His ways, but still they often sinned and turned against Him. Yet God always loved them and always wanted to forgive them no matter how often they turned away.  Hosea 11:8–9

# E XERCISES

1.   What kind of people were the Israelites?
2.   What was God like?
3.   Why did the Israelites turn back to God?
4.   What is the similarity between the way God treated the Israelites and the way Mr Ryan treated Joseph? Are there any differences?

> To forgive means to love people even when they have sinned, and to give them another chance to be loving. God never stops loving us, no matter what we do. God is always waiting for us to ask His forgiveness so that He can help us to be loving people again. Because God forgives us, He asks us to forgive one another.

5. Describe an occasion when you needed forgiveness. Who forgave you? Explain.

6. Describe an occasion when you forgave someone. Did you find it easy? Explain.

*Reflection*: 'The Lord is merciful and loving, slow to become angry and full of constant love.' Psalm 103:8

*Action*: Prepare and act out a drama about forgiveness. You could work in groups and produce a mini Drama Festival for your school.

*Song*: 'Oh the Love of My Lord is the Essence'

*Prayer*: Oh Lord, we thank you for offering your forgiveness before we even ask. (*Pause to remember our sins.*) We praise you for your never-ending love. Amen.

# FAMILY

## CHAPTER 12

**The Turnip Family Game**
*(See instructions on next page.)*

BABY
BRIAN

GRANNY

SISTER
SARAH

AUNTIE
ANNIE

COUSIN
CLAIRE

GRAND
UNCLE
HUMPHREY

BROTHER
BRENDAN

## Instructions

*The aim of the game is*

(a) to collect as many family member cards as possible, by landing on the family member spaces, and

(b) to get as many family points as you can.

*Time limit: 20 minutes.*

*You will need:*

1. One set of family member cards for each player. Each set should include all of the family members shown on the board overleaf. You can make the cards from stiff paper or cardboard.

2. One dice for each group of players. There should be no more than four players in each group.

3. One counter or token for each player.

4. A large sheet of paper, a ruler and a pen. These are for the scorekeeper, one of the group of players. If you are the scorekeeper, write 'Family Points' at the top of the sheet of paper. Then divide the sheet into columns, using ruler and pen. Write one player's name over each column. Don't forget to include your own name. When any player gets a family point, you write in the score under that player's name.

*How to play:*

1. Put all the sets of family member cards in the middle of the table. This is the deck.

2. Use one person's religion book as the board.

3. Each player rolls the dice. The player with the highest score starts. When the first player has finished his/her turn, the player immediately to his/her left has the next turn, and so on.

4. You start by putting your counter or token on any family member space on the board. You can then take that family member card from the deck. For example, if you put your token on Granny Turnip, then you can take a Granny card from the deck.

5. Roll the dice and move your token the correct number of spaces in any direction. Each player gets only one roll of the dice per turn.

6. If you land on a blue square, you immediately get *three* family points.

7. If you land on a red square, you get *one* family point, but only if you give an example to show how you could try to make a member of your own family happy. If you do not give an example, you do not get a point. (Players may not repeat an example already given by themselves or by another player.)

8. The first time you land on a family member space, you can take a card corresponding to that member from the deck. You cannot get another card for the same family member, even if you land on that space again.

9. Your turn always ends when you reach a family member space.

*The winner*

1. At the end of the game, the scorekeeper adds up the points in each player's family points column.

2. The winner is the player with the most family member cards, regardless of how many family points he/she has.

3. If two or more people have the same number of family member cards, then the winner is the person with the highest family points score among them.

# *Q*UESTION

1. If you played the Turnip Family Game, you may have noticed that this family has a great variety of people in it. Can you think of any ways in which the Turnip family could make each other happy because they are so different? Could their differences lead to problems for them? Explain.

# *E*XERCISES

1. In what ways is your family similar to the Turnip family? In what ways is it different?
2. In the game, the way to get a lot of family points was to go the long way around and take time using the black squares. If you were in a rush to get family member cards, you may not have got many family points. If your family is always in a rush, and too busy to talk to each other, could this lead to problems? Explain.

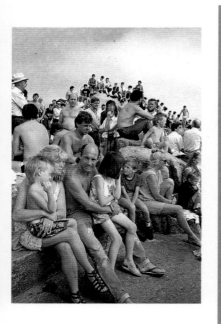

Every family is different, whether there are two or twenty people in it. A family is the community most people know best. Like all communities, families have good and bad points, strengths and weaknesses. Many families have special problems: the illness or handicap of one or more members; personality clashes; unemployment; not enough living space; or having to live apart from one another. These and other problems can make life very difficult at times. Despite this fact, most people wouldn't change their family for anything. There is something special about belonging to a family community. The closeness experienced between brothers, sisters, parents, guardians, uncles, aunts or grannies is difficult to find outside the family circle. God gives us families because He loves us, and wants us to love one another so that we will be happy. All families fail to love each other at times, and so we must learn to forgive one another. It is important for families to pray together and ask God to help them to love each other better.

# EXERCISES

1. A community is a group of people working together to achieve a common aim. They help each other and care for one another as much as they can. Why do we call the family a community?
2. Describe three ways in which you showed your love for your family last week.
3. How did the members of your family show they loved you last week?
4. Can you think of any way in which you fail to love a member of your family? What are the effects of this sin? How could you change?
5. Do you remember a time when someone in your family forgave you for something? How did you feel? Explain.
6. How and when do families celebrate together? What effects can these celebrations have on the family?

*Reflection*: 'Do not use harmful words, but only helpful words, the kind that build up and provide what is needed, so that what you say will do good to those who hear you.' Ephesians 4:29

*Action*: Make a big poster showing all the things you like about being part of your family. Display it at home where everyone in the family can see it. If some members of your family are living away from home, send them a postcard or letter telling them about the poster.

*Song*: 'Love'

*Prayer*: Dear God, we thank you for our families. Bless them, and help all family members to love and forgive one another, so that everyone will be happy as you have planned. Amen.

# SCRIPTURE – THE OLD TESTAMENT

## THE BIBLE

### CHAPTER 13

▼

The Farrells were moving — emigrating in fact. Both parents had lost their jobs when the textile factory had closed down over a year ago. Neither had been able to get work since. A friend had recently got jobs for them in Coventry, England. Like their parents, fifteen-year-old Laura and Declan, aged thirteen, were sad to be leaving their home town, their friends and relations, but they were excited too. In one way, it would be a great adventure. Meanwhile, the business of moving house was taking every minute of the day, it seemed.

While they were clearing out the attic, Declan came across a strong cardboard box full of paper, copies, scrapbooks and old photograph albums. He took out a copy with 'Declan Farrell, First Class' written on the front. The writing was large and un-even. Inside were spelling tests, 'news' paragraphs, and brightly coloured matchstick people.

'Hey Mam,' he shouted, 'Look what I've found.' He carried the box down to the sitting-room.

Soon everyone was pulling out long-forgotten possessions. There were ancient photographs of First Holy Communions, Confirmations, weddings, holidays, friends and relations. There was a photograph of a two-month-old Declan having a bath.

'Yeuch,' said Declan in disgust.

There was a battered notebook of poems which Laura had written in primary school. 'I thought they had been thrown out years ago,' she exclaimed, embarrassed.

'Certainly not,' said her father, grinning. 'I'm not going to throw away the evidence that my daughter is a poet.'

'Oh, Dad,' groaned Laura. 'Just don't show them to anyone.' Then her face brightened: 'Look what's down at the bottom — my old gym trophies.'

Declan found an old hurley ball; his mother found her scrapbooks, full of bits and pieces cut from newspapers and magazines; his father picked out the diaries he had kept over the years, some from his schooldays. There were loads of Christmas and birthday cards, and old letters.

'What are we going to do with all this stuff?' asked Laura. 'Throw it out?'

'Oh no. We'll have to take it with us,' said Declan.

'But why? What good is it?' said his sister.

'I don't know,' he answered. 'It's just — interesting. We'll probably forget most of it if we don't keep the letters and photos and things.

'I agree,' said his mother. 'It's easy to forget even important things. There's a letter here from Uncle Colm. He lent us the money for the deposit on this house, you know. Only for him we'd still have been living in that pokey flat when Laura was born. We paid him back, of course, but we haven't even written to him for over ten years. We should have kept in touch — he was a good friend.'

'We'll write to him tonight,' said her husband.

'See?' said Declan, looking triumphantly at Laura. 'That's one good thing that's come from all this stuff.'

'Oh, have it your own way,' said Laura.

So Declan took charge of the 'family box'. He thought it was very interesting to see the kind of person he had been years ago, and be reminded of all the things that had happened to him. It seemed odd to him, but also fascinating, to think of his parents living their own lives before he was born, before anyone had known he would ever exist. Some day, he thought, he would put all the main things into a book, or even make a video of them. Then they could never be left behind in an attic and maybe lost forever. He couldn't explain even to himself why this was so important to him, but it seemed even more vital because the family was going to England. They might never return to live in Ireland. It would be good for future generations of Farrells to know the kind of people their ancestors had been, and it would be good to be remembered.

41

# QUESTIONS

1.  What sort of things did the Farrell family find in the box?
2.  Why did they want to keep these things?
3.  Do most families keep things like old letters, cards or photographs? Why? Why not? Do you keep things like this? Why? Why not? Describe them if you do.
4.  Are there any advantages in keeping such things?
5.  Would you have thrown out the box? Why? Why not?

God's chosen people are one large family. The most important thing about His people is that God loves them and wants them to share a special relationship with Him. In some ways the Bible is like a 'family box' belonging to God's chosen people. The contents remind us about all the wonderful things God has done for His people since the beginning of time. It also tells us how the people reacted to God. Like any family story, it is partly happy, partly sad, sometimes violent, often funny.

In some ways the Bible is different to an ordinary collection of family keepsakes. In the Bible, God tells us what He will do for *us* now and in the future, as well as what He has done in the past for His people. The Bible contains human dramas, poems and short stories (like the ones you might study in English or French) as well as history, prayers and warnings. For example in Genesis 22:1–13, we can read the story of how God tested Abraham. In Acts 2:1–4 we can read what happened when God sent the Holy Spirit to the Apostles. All of these tell us about God's work in our world, God's relationship with individual people and with communities. By reading the Bible we can also find out about God's plan for us today, as members of His family.

# EXERCISES

1.  Name some of God's chosen people who are mentioned in the Bible.
2.  Do you remember how God showed His love for any of these people? Explain.

3. How did the people respond to God in each of the situations you have mentioned?
4. Do you know any of the dramas, poems or stories from the Bible? Describe one if you can.
5. What does your story tell us about God?
6. Does it tell you anything about God's plan for us?

*Reflection*: 'All Scripture is inspired by God and is useful for teaching the truth, rebuking error, correcting faults, and giving instruction for right living, so that the person who serves God may be fully qualified and equipped to do every kind of good deed.' 2 Timothy 3:16–17

*Song*: 'Sing to the Lord'

*Prayer*: Thank you Lord for giving us the Bible. Help us to know and understand its message. Amen.

# DISCOVERING GOD'S LOVE
# IN THE BIBLE

## CHAPTER 14

Elaine was doing a project on zoos. She had some information, but wanted more. 'Why not try the encyclopedia?' said her teacher. So off she went to the library and began to search. Ten hours later she was fed up. 'There's nothing about the zoo in these encyclopedias,' she announced to the librarian in disgust. 'I've already looked through A, B, C, D, E, and F and there's nothing of any use in them.'

Alan was thrilled with his new computer. He was looking forward to playing games on it, and maybe getting some help with his homework as well. He decided to test it out with a few questions. He plugged the computer in and switched on. Then with one finger he typed: 'What is the capital of France?' The computer gave no answer. He tried again: 2 + 2 = ? The screen was still blank. 'Stupid machine,' he said, and walked off.

## QUESTIONS

1. What advice would you give Elaine? Why?
2. What advice would you give Alan? Why?

There is a lot of information in books, videos, computers, and tapes. If we don't know how to use a tape, then it is just a lump of plastic.
If we know how to look up a particular book, we can find out what we want to know.

## EXERCISES

1. Pretend you are going to do a project on sport. List all the different methods you could use in looking for information.
2. Compare your answers with the rest of the class.

We need to know how to use the Bible in order to benefit fully from it.

The Bible is divided into two Sections.

**Old Testament** is the story of the Chosen People before Jesus was born.

**New Testament** is the story of Jesus and his message, and how he called the Christian community together.

Between them, the two testaments contain seventy-two books.

After centuries of use people found it was more useful to divide the books of the Bible into sections. This made it easier to find the different stories and teachings.

Today, each book is divided into *chapters*.

**Genesis**
Chapter 1  In the beginning . . .
Chapter 2 . . .

Each chapter is divided into *verses*.
**Genesis**
Chapter 18  1  And the Lord appeared to . . .
            2 . . .
            3 . . .
            4 . . .
            5 . . .
            6 . . .
            7 . . .

# SSIGNMENT

1.  Make sure you can find the Old Testament and the New Testament in the Bible.
2.  Find the Book of Genesis in the Old Testament (hint: it is the first book of the Bible). Genesis is often written as 'Gen'.
3.  Find Chapter 1 in the Book of Genesis. This is usually written as  Gen 1.
4.  Find verse 31 in Gen 1.
5.  Write out the verse in your copy.
    If ever you need to find this verse again you simply look up the Book of Genesis: chapter 1: verse 31.  The short form is: Gen 1:31. Gen 1:31 is called a Reference to the Bible.
6.  See if you can find the following references in the Old Testament:        (a) Gen 2:4–9
    (b) Gen 12:1–7        (c) Exodus (Ex) 3:1–12.
7.  Write or draw an account of each of these three Bible references.
8.  How does God show His love for His people in each of these references?
9.  How do the people respond?

*Reflection*: 'Never forget these commands that I am giving you today. Teach them to your children. Repeat them when you are at home and when you are away, when you are resting and when you are working. Tie them on your arms and wear them on your foreheads as a reminder. Write them on the door-posts of your houses and on your gates.' Deuteronomy 6:6–9

*Action*: Make up a quiz based on references to the Bible.
*Example*: What person is mentioned in Mark 1:6?
*Answer*: John the Baptist.

    Each person in the class should take a different book of the Bible, and make up five to 10 questions like this. Each question should be on a different piece of paper. Put all the questions into a box. The teacher or a student can be the questioner. Divide the class into teams, with one Bible per person. When a question is asked, the first team to get the right answer gets 2 points. The team with the most points at the end wins.

*Song*: 'Glory to God'

*Prayer*: We praise you, oh Lord, for speaking to us through your word.  Amen.

# GOD'S LOVE IN THE COMMANDMENTS

## CHAPTER 15

Examine the following situations carefully. In each case the main character has a choice about how to act, and one of the commandments (on the next page) could help the person to make a loving decision. You have to work out (i) what choices does the person have in each situation, and (ii) which commandment most applies in each case.

1.  Joan's best friend has lots of other friends besides Joan, and sometimes goes places with them without Joan.
2.  John's baby brother has just broken John's new record. John is very angry.
3.  At the moment the only thing in Alan's life is football. Nothing is allowed to interfere with the training, matches or watching the game on TV.
4.  Niamh's birthday is two days after Kate's. Kate always gets far better and more expensive presents, because she has older brothers and sisters.
5.  Elaine hardly notices any more when she uses the name of God or Jesus in casual conversation.
6.  The boys in Colm's class often snigger and jeer at the girls they meet going home from school.
7.  Sharon wants to go to the disco with Ruth, but her parents think she's too young. Ruth suggests that Sharon ask her parents if she may 'stay for the night' at Ruth's house, and then she and Sharon can go.
8.  Jim's parents have a hard job getting him out to last Mass on a Sunday. Sometimes he doesn't make it.
9.  Colette thinks her parents are OK, but her friends often give out about their parents, and expect her to join in.
10. David's mother gave him a £10 note to get some groceries. In the shop he discovers he actually has two £10 notes stuck together.

God rescued His people from Egypt, and led them through the desert to the promised land. Because He loved them so much, He gave His commandments at Mount Sinai. These commands were God's guidelines to His people. By obeying these guidelines, the people would be following God's plan for them. This plan was that they would get to know and love God, and love each other as a community. The first three commandments would help them to love God by putting Him first in their lives, by treating Him with respect, and by setting aside one day a week in which to worship God in a special way. The last seven commandments would help them to love each other better, by turning away from violence, greed, envy and dishonesty, all of which can destroy love and happiness.

# EXERCISE

1. Write out the commandments and learn them.

*Reflection*: 'For this is the love of God that we keep His commandments. And His commandments are not burdensome.' 1 John 5:3

*Action*: Make up a drama based on one of the commandments. Show in the drama that following the commandment helps people to love God and each other better in either the family, class or school. (You might divide into groups, each group taking a different commandment.)

*Song*: 'Yahweh, I Know You Are Near'

*Prayer*: Thank you Lord for your commandments, your guidance and your help. Amen.

# RULES IN MY LIFE

## CHAPTER 16

Divide the class into groups. Each group is to do the following exercise.

A new youth club has been set up in your area. You are on the committee of young people who are going to be responsible for organising the club. No adults will be involved unless the committee asks for them. You have been given the use of a big old house, on two acres of land, for the club. The house has one large hall, and eight other big rooms, two bathrooms, a kitchen, and some sheds at the back. There are some chairs and tables, but no other furniture in the house. With the other people on the committee you must decide:

(a) How the club will be organised
(b) What activities will take place
(c) What rules (if any) there will be
(d) What fund-raising will be needed.

Each group should report back to the class. Can the class come to an overall agreement?

The purpose of rules is to make life happier for people, especially when they are living, working or enjoying themselves together in groups. All good rules follow God's guidelines, so that they can help us to be happy as God has planned.

# QUESTIONS

1.  How would your rules for the youth club help the club to be better?
2.  How would the club have been affected if there were no rules?
3.  Can you discover any links between your rules for the club and God's commandments to us?

Most of us live and work in communities all of the time — at home, school, and with friends. In each of these communities we often find rules that other people have made for us to follow.

# EXERCISES

1.  What rules do you find helpful:
    (a) at home
    (b) at school
    (c) among friends?
    Explain.
2.  Which rules do you see as unhelpful in each of these communities? Why?
3.  Do you think God's commandments are taken into account in the rules you have to follow in your life? Explain.

*Reflection*: 'Rules for friendship: "Whoever betrays secrets destroys confidence, and he will never find a congenial friend. Love your friend and keep faith with him; but if you betray his secrets, do not run after him. For as a man destroys his enemy, so you have destroyed the friendship of your neighbour. And as you allow a bird to escape from your hand, so you have let your neighbour go and will not catch him again. Do not go after him, for he is too far off, and has escaped like a gazelle from a snare. For a wound may be bandaged, and there is reconciliation after abuse, but whoever has betrayed secrets is without hope."' Sirach 27:16–21

*Action*: Examine your school rules. Could you add any extra rules which would help your school to be a more loving community?

*Song*: 'Christ Be Beside Me'

*Prayer*: Lord, help us to obey all good rules so that we may be happier together in our communities. Amen.

# A NEW COMMANDMENT

## CHAPTER 17

▼

### QUESTIONS

1. What are the similarities between the two cartoon strips?
2. What are the differences between them?
3. Which of the ten commandments applies to both of these situations?

When Jesus lived on earth, he followed all of the ten commandments. In his dealings with the people he met, Jesus was honest and respectful. He did not just love those he knew well, he actually loved everybody. He loved his followers in a special way, and he gave them a new commandment: to love each other as he loved them. All members of the Christian community are called by Jesus to obey this commandment.

In the cartoons it is obvious which of the boys obeyed Jesus' new commandment. It is also clear that this made a difference to his family life.

# EXERCISES

1. Carefully examine the following two situations:
   (a) Your mother's purse is on the table. No one is around. You want to buy sweets, but you have no money.
   (b) Your mother asks you, 'Have you done your homework?' and you say 'Yes,' even though you haven't done your maths.
   (i) In each case say which of the ten commandments could be used as a guideline for action.
   (ii) Would the actions be any different in each case if Jesus' new commandment was followed?

2. Now think about these examples.
   (a) Your sister wishes to borrow your new bicycle, but you don't want anyone else to use it.
   (b) You've heard an unpleasant rumour about another student in your class, and you're dying to share the rumour with your friends.
   (i) Would any of the ten commandments help you to decide what to do in situations (a) or (b) above? Explain your answer.
   (ii) Do you think Jesus' new commandment would be more helpful? Why? Why not?

# GROUP WORK

1. When you have done this work on your own, form groups of four or five in the class and compare your answers. Can you come to an agreement? Report back to the whole class.

If we love one another as Jesus asked us to do, we will try to think of other people and how they feel. We will try to act in a way that will make our communities at home, at school and in our neighbourhood a better place to live in.

# EXERCISES

1.  Write down the names of three people you meet each day. Make a list of the ways you might be more loving towards them by following Jesus' commandment.
2.  Your class is a community. Give three examples of how you could improve that community by following Jesus' commandment.

*Reflection*: 'Be under obligation to no one — the only obligation you have is to love one another. Whoever does this has obeyed the Law. The commandments, 'Do not commit adultery; do not commit murder; do not steal; do not desire what belongs to someone else' — all these, and any others besides, are summed up in the one command, 'Love your neighbour as you love yourself.' If you love someone, you will never do him wrong; to love, then, is to obey the whole Law.' Romans 13:8–10

*Action*:  The Happy Circle
1.  Write your name at the top of a page.
2.  Underneath your name write down at least one thing you think makes *you* a loving person.
3.  Divide the class into *four* groups of 7 or 8. Each group to sit in a circle.
4.  Pass your page to the person on your right.
5.  You will have in front of you the page belonging to the person on your left. Write down one thing which you like about that person, something which makes them a loving person.
6.  When everyone has written a comment, again pass the paper you have to the person on your right.
7.  Continue in this fashion until you have written a comment on everyone's sheet of paper. You should now have got your own sheet back. This page is an account of your good qualities, of what makes you a loving person. Congratulations!

*Song*: 'Love is His Word'

*Prayer*: Lord Jesus, we thank you for showing us how to love one another. Help us to follow your example every day. Amen.

# UNIT IV

# THE NEW TESTAMENT — JESUS

## JESUS' LIFE IN PALESTINE

### CHAPTER 18

**The World of the New Testament**

Jesus lived in Palestine, a region at the eastern end of the Mediterranean Sea. The climate was generally sunny and warm, though it could get very cold at night. Most of the area on this map was ruled by the Romans.

## QUESTIONS

1. Can you find the following places on the map?
   (a) Palestine
   (b) Jerusalem — the capital city of Judea
   (c) Rome — the capital city of the entire Roman Empire.

2. Can you pick out any place names on the map that might be mentioned on the news today?

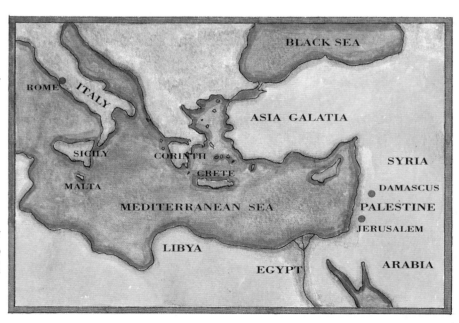

3. Examine the map on this page carefully, then see if you can find the following:
   (a) The town where Jesus was born
   (b) The town in which he lived
   (c) The city in which Jesus preached and eventually was crucified
   (d) The lake where Jesus went fishing with his apostles.

▲ *Fishing at dawn on Lake Galilee*

▲ *The Golan heights in Galilee today*

▲ *Street market in Nazareth today*

▲ *Inside the oldest synagogue in North Africa today. It has changed little from the time of Jesus.*

SYRIA

GALILEE

CAPERNAUM

LAKE GALILEE

NAZARETH

MEDITERRANEAN SEA

SAMARIA

JORDAN RIVER

JERUSALEM

BETHLEHEM

JUDEA

DEAD SEA

▲ *Soldiers, carved on an ancient Roman monument*

▲ *Model of the Temple in Jerusalem at the time of Jesus*

57

4. Describe the countryside of Galilee where Jesus lived for most of his life.
5. How did many of the people of Galilee make their living?
6. How did Jesus and Joseph make their living?

▲
*The Mezuzah*

At this time Palestine was part of the Roman Empire. Even in faraway Nazareth Jesus would have seen many Roman soldiers. Joseph would have paid heavy taxes to the local tax collector appointed by the Romans. The tax collectors were often local Jews. The people saw them as traitors and hated them.

The Romans appointed rulers to govern the different parts of Palestine. During Jesus' lifetime the ruler of Galilee was King Herod. Pontius Pilate was the Roman responsible for that part of Palestine called Judea.

Jesus was born into a Jewish family. Their religion was very important to the Jews. They tried to keep God's commandments and prayed daily. The Jews loved God's word in the Scriptures (what we now call the Old Testament). On the doorpost of every Jewish home there was a 'mezuzah'. This was a container with a parchment scroll inside. Some of the most important Scripture verses were written on this special parchment.

There was also a full copy of the Scriptures in the local synagogue where the people came to worship. Jesus probably went to the synagogue each Sabbath day to pray with the rest of his community. Every Jew living in Palestine tried to make a pilgrimage three times a year to the temple at Jerusalem. Jesus first made this pilgrimage at the age of twelve, as was the custom.

There were many Jewish festivals celebrated by all the people, like the Passover, and the Festival of Lights.

*A Jewish family celebrates the Seder meal* ▶

The Jews did not agree on all matters of religion among themselves. Jesus would have known some Pharisees, Sadducees and probably some Samaritans. The Pharisees believed that by following strict laws in every tiny detail of their lives they would come closer to God. The Sadducees also tried to follow the law, but were not as strict as the Pharisees. The people of Samaria (Samaritans), while they had many of the same beliefs as the Jews, practised their religion in a different way. For example, they did not worship at the Temple in Jerusalem. The Jews and the Samaritans despised each other.

# GROUP WORK

1. Are there any similarities between your daily life and Jesus' life in Nazareth?
2. What are the major differences?

*Reflection*: 'So Jesus went back with them to Nazareth, where he was obedient to them . . . Jesus grew both in body and in wisdom, gaining favour with God and men.' Luke 2:51, 52

*Action*: Find out all you can about life in Galilee today. (It is now part of Israel.) Ask your parents, read newspapers, listen to the news for information. Make a note of what you find.

*Song*: 'Lord of the Dance'

*Prayer*: Lord Jesus, when you lived on earth you were like us in all things except sin. So you understand all our worries and joys. Help us to realise how near you are to us at all times. Amen.

# JESUS CALLS
# A COMMUNITY

## CHAPTER 19
▼

▲
*The banks of the Jordan river*

*Dear Jacob,*
Greetings!

Wonderful news. We have found the Messiah, yes truly! We were at the Jordan river as usual, when Jesus of Nazareth arrived. Apparently John (the Baptist) had baptised him in the river some time before, but this was the first time I had seen him.

John pointed him out to us saying that Jesus is actually the Saviour. Some of us, including my brother Simon, have already joined Jesus' group, with John's blessing. Jesus has asked us to come with him to Galilee. He is teaching us how to live as a community so that we will be ready to be part of the Kingdom of God. Jesus says that what God asks of us is that we love Him and each other. Soon we will be sent out in Jesus' name to bring others into his community.

If you can possibly get away, you should try to come to Galilee and hear him teach. I have never met anyone quite like him. When you hear him you will understand what I mean.

Your friend,
Andrew

*Dear Joachim,*
Greetings from Galilee.

What am I doing in Galilee, I hear you ask? You will find this difficult to believe, but I have become the follower of a Nazarene. Yes, I know what you'll say, 'What good can come out of Nazareth?' That's just what I said to Philip when he came rushing in to tell me that he had found the Messiah. Joachim, I am convinced that Jesus really is the Son of God.

He has miraculous powers. I've seen them, Joachim! Some paralysed! Others blind and pitiful or deaf and dumb! But when he touches them they are completely cured. No one could have such power unless they came from God. These are great days, Joachim, great days.

Nathaniel

**Dear Anna,**

Greetings to you and to all the family. I write in the hope that you could send Joseph down to me for a few weeks to help on the boats. My smart boys have taken it into their heads to become 'fishers of men' instead of plain fishermen. A travelling preacher from Nazareth (of all places!) has completely dazzled James and John.

First, they started going to Capernaum to hear him preach in the synagogue. Then, they started talking to him and his followers and not coming home until all hours. But then, just when I was getting some work out of them down at the beach, up he comes and asks them to be his followers. And the two of them drop everything and head off.

Their mother says they'll come to their senses after a few days of sleeping rough. I certainly hope so! Meanwhile, I have to take on extra help for the boats. Young Joseph would be a great help if you can spare him.

▲ *Lakeside in Galilee*

Your brother,<br/>Zebedee

**Dear Martha,**

Just a quick message to let you know how things are going. I am sending this letter with Baruch, bless him. Martha, I have never known such peace and happiness. There is quite a large group of us now following the Lord. Not all can leave their homes of course, but they are trying to live the message of Jesus whilst going about their daily lives.

Those of us who are lucky enough to meet with Jesus every day, eat with him, and hear his teachings, are blessed indeed. He makes no distinctions between people like Joanna, the wife of Herod's steward who is wealthy, and Mary, who has nothing. In fact he asks that all of us treat each other as brothers and sisters. This is not easy as you may imagine, since we are a mixed bunch! But somehow when Jesus is there, everything seems possible.

I praise the Lord that I have lived to see this day.

Your friend,<br/>Suzanna

*To Jonas, Greetings!*

Another one of those wandering preachers is in the area. Jesus, son of Joseph, a carpenter from Nazareth, I believe. Some of the common people think he's the Messiah. I am very concerned about this. They leave their homes and go tramping after him, or they stay at home and sing his praises from morning till night.

Some of the other scribes think he might be dangerous. I am not afraid of his influence, but if he continues to fill the people's heads with nonsense, something will have to be done to stop him. He actually takes his meals with tax collectors and other sinners! He encourages his followers to do the same. He'd better move on soon and take his followers with him.

Your fellow scribe,
Bartholomew

*Dear John,*

I just had to write to tell you of the way in which my life has changed. You remember I told you that no-one in the village would talk to me because of my job. Nobody loves a tax collector! But, believe it or not, there are now some people in the village who smile and greet me warmly — I feel like a human being again! It is all because of this man, Jesus of Nazareth, who makes even tax collectors welcome in his community of followers. My life will never be the same again. I have even stopped cheating people when they pay their taxes.

Seth

Jesus lived quietly for thirty years in Nazareth; then he began his public life as a wandering preacher. To mark the beginning of his preaching life Jesus was baptised in the Jordan river by John the Baptist. (Mark 1:9)

Afterwards he went away to fast and pray by himself in the wilderness of Judea to prepare for his work. Then Jesus went back to Galilee and began to preach. From the beginning it was clear that Jesus was different. His message was very clear. He told people, 'the right time has come and the Kingdom of God is near, turn away from your sins and believe the Good News.' People listened to Jesus with growing interest. His stories fascinated them. He spoke about the wayward son and the good father (Luke 16:1–9) and held them spellbound with his stories of the Kingdom of Heaven (Luke 14:16–24). He amazed them by curing the blind people (Mark 8:22–26) and paralysed people (Mark 2:3–5). They were thrilled by the way in which he stood up to the Pharisees. Many people answered Jesus' call and became his followers. Fishermen and tax collectors, rich and poor people, old and young, all were welcomed by Jesus. Some people like the scribes and the Pharisees were jealous of Jesus, and wanted to get rid of him.

# EXERCISES

Read carefully the letters on the previous pages and answer the following questions:

1. What message did Jesus have for the people?
2. How did the people of Palestine react to Jesus and his message?
3. What kind of people did Jesus ask to join his community?
4. How were the people in the community supposed to treat each other?
5. What difference did it make to them to be members of Jesus' community?

> Jesus asked his followers to spread his message and bring other people into his community. We are part of this community today. Jesus calls us to live and work together as his followers, and we in our turn are asked to call others.

6. What message does Jesus have for us today?
7. How do we react to Jesus and his message?
8. What kind of people does Jesus ask to join his community?
9. How are the people in our community supposed to treat each other?
10. What difference does it make to us to be members of Jesus' community?

*Reflection*: 'And Jesus said: "I have been given all authority in heaven and on earth. Go, then, to all people everywhere and make them my disciples: baptise them in the name of the Father, the Son, and the Holy Spirit, and teach them to obey everything I have commanded you. And I will be with you always, to the end of the age."' Matthew 28:18–20

*Action*: Think of any action you could perform which would encourage another person to become a member of Jesus' community.

*Song*: 'The Spirit of the Lord'

*Prayer*: Dear Lord Jesus, thank you for calling us to be part of your community. Help us to turn away from our sins and work with you to spread the Good News. Amen.

# PARABLES

## CHAPTER 20

At the local youth club some of the boys and girls were sitting around grumbling about how they were treated at home. 'It's so unfair,' Elaine was saying. 'Just because I'm the eldest in my family, I get left with everything. If the dishes are left in the sink, or the grass isn't cut, I get the blame.'

'Same here,' said John. 'If you're the eldest you're always in trouble.'

Séamus laughed bitterly. Just be grateful you're not the youngest. At least you two are allowed to go places and do interesting things. If I want to go to a film or the disco, I'm told I'm far too young.

A youth club leader was listening to the comments and after a while he said, 'Have any of you heard the story of the poor man who went to the wise old man to ask for help?'

'What story is that?' asked Elaine.

'Well, this poor man went to the wise man and said, "Old man, I'm desperate. There are ten of us — ten — in one miserable room. Can you imagine the over-crowding, the constant noise, the continual fighting? When one of us sneezes, another says 'excuse me!' Wise old man, what shall I do?"

'The wise man was silent. Finally he said, "You own a goat?"

'"Yes," answered the poor man, rather surprised.

'"Bring the goat into the room to live with you," said the wise man.

'"But surely . . ." cried the man.

'"And come back to me in a week," the wise old man said. The poor man went home to follow the wise man's advice.

'The following week he returned. "Well," said the wise old man, "Is everything going well at home?"

'"Everything is ten times worse," wailed the man. "It's that goat in the room — she's unbearable. There is even less space for all of us than before and the room is filthy — the smell is disgusting. The goat keeps eating everything — our clothes,

our food, our shoes — and she is deafening us with her bleating. Please use your wisdom to think of something else we can do!"

'The wise old man was silent for a moment. Then he said, "Put the goat back in her shed."

'"Is that all?" asked the man.

'"And come back to me in a week," said the wise man.

'Exactly one week later the poor man returned. "Well," said the wise old man, "Is everything going well at home?"

'"Everything is wonderful, wonderful, old man. There's no smell, everything is sparkling clean. Our charming room is such a pleasant place to be, with just the ten of us in it! How can we ever thank you enough?"

When the leader had finished, the group laughed, and John said, 'OK, we get the message! Being the eldest may be bad, but it could be worse, so let's be grateful for what we've got.'

'I suppose being the youngest does have it's advantages,' said Séamus. 'At least I don't have to do any babysitting!'

'There's just one problem now,' said Elaine solemnly. 'What on earth are we going to talk about now that we can't complain any more?'

'Trust you to think of that one!' said the youth leader.

# *Q*UESTIONS

1. What do you think was the message of the story told by the youth leader?
2. Why do you think the leader told the group a story, rather than discussing their complaints with them, for example?
3. Did the young people change their opinions in any way because of the story?
4. Do you think the young people would change their actions in any way because of the story? Why? Why not?

Sometimes people tell us stories just to entertain us. Adventure films or detective books are based on this kind of story. Other stories are told so that we will learn something and be entertained at the same time. Films about World War Two or nature programmes are examples of this kind of story. Some stories are told to make us think and they can change the way we think or act. The story told by the youth leader was a parable. His aim was to help the young people to think a bit more: he wanted them to stop grumbling and complaining and realise how well off they were. The parable helped the young people to change.

A parable is a story which is told to make people think and it can change the way people think or act.

# QUESTIONS

1. Can you think of any parables you were ever told, perhaps by a parent or teacher?
2. Did the parable actually help you change? Why/Why not?

Many of Jesus' stories were parables which got people thinking. He told them to people he met to help them change their views about other people and about God. Jesus also speaks to us today through the parables in the Gospels. When we read them, Jesus asks us to change the way we think and act so that we will be the kind of people God wants us to be. Through the parables we can find out more about ourselves; we see what kind of people we can become; and our relationship with God and others can be changed.

3. Read St Luke, Chapter 15.
   (a) What did the Pharisees and the teachers of the law think about tax collectors and outcasts? How did they treat them?
   (b) According to the Pharisees, who would be more important to God, the tax collectors or themselves?
   (c) Read Luke 15:4–7 again. In this parable, how does Jesus try to change the Pharisees' opinions about (i) the outcasts, and (ii) God?

(d) Read Luke 15:8–10 again. In this parable, how does Jesus try to change the Pharisees' opinions about (i) the outcasts, and (ii) God?

(e) Read Luke 15:11–32 again. In this parable, how does Jesus try to change the Pharisees' views about (i) God, and (ii) themselves?

4.  Imagine that Jesus is telling these stories to your class today.

(a) Are there any groups of people who are sometimes regarded as outcasts in our society? (For example, poor people, prisoners)

(b) How do we think about these people, and how are they treated?

(c) In the parable you have chosen, how does Jesus suggest we change our views of these groups?

# ASSIGNMENT

Make a poster for your classroom or school based on one of the above parables, or on one of the following parables: Matthew 20:1–6, Mark 4:1–9 and 13–20, Luke 18:9–14, Matthew 18:21–35. Remember — your poster should encourage the people who see it to change their thinking or their actions!

*Reflection*: 'I have taught you wisdom and the right way to live. Nothing will stand in your way if you walk wisely, and you will not stumble when you run. Always remember what you have learnt. Your education is your life — guard it well.' Proverbs 4:11–13

*Action*: Working alone or in small groups, prepare a poster project based on one or more of the parables, and arrange to display it somewhere in your local community — the community hall, the shopping centre or the church.

*Song*: 'Song of Good News'

*Prayer*: Lord Jesus, we thank you for your gift of the parables. By listening to and reflecting on them, may we become loving, happy people. Amen.

# SIGNS

## CHAPTER 21

▼

**Word Puzzle**

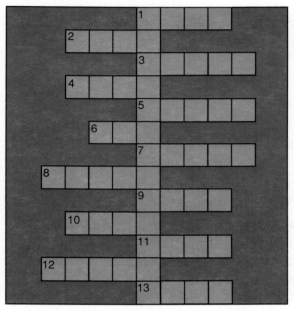

*Clues Down:*

1.

*Clues Across:*

1.

2.

3.

4.

5.

6.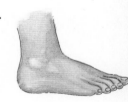

7.

8.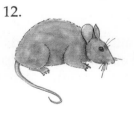

9.

10.

11.

12.

13.

If you were able to complete the word puzzle on the previous page, then you are good at following signs.

> A sign is any word, action or picture that gives a message which everyone can understand.

# EXERCISES

1. Draw any sign that you might see in each of the following places:
    (a) In school
    (b) At home
    (c) In the shops
    (d) On the roads.
Carefully explain what each of your four signs mean.

2. (a) AGAPAO       (b) R       (c)

If you speak Greek, the meaning of (a) is simple; it means 'I love'.

If you know the 'Rules of the Road' for Northern Ireland, you will know that (b) means 'restricted driver'.

If you see (c) on a garment label, it means 'Do not wash'.

3. What does exercise 2 tell us about signs?

# ASSIGNMENT

Make a list of some religious signs. Draw them if you can. Explain what they mean.

*Reflection*: 'And this is what will prove it to you: you will find a baby wrapped in strips of cloth and lying in a manger.' Luke 2:12

*Action*: Go to your local church and find three signs which show that it is a Christian church.

*Song*: 'Like a Shepherd'

*Prayer*: Lord Jesus, your healing hands and powerful words show us that you love all humanity. Help us to get to know and love you better through your signs. Amen.

# SYMBOLS

## CHAPTER 22

### The Flick Knife

Reverend Tom Jarvie was a minister in a big city. His church stood among tenements and grim, grey factories. Many youngsters who passed its door were aimless and trouble-seeking. Mr Jarvie made it his business to reach out and welcome them to his church and youth club.

Some were involved with gangs, and they hoped to break up the good work Mr Jarvie had started. But he had come up the hard way too. And soon the scoffers and trouble-makers found themselves respecting him and what he stood for.

So much so, that one day one of the teenage gang leaders asked to see him alone. Earnestly, Johnny told the minister he had come to the crossroads. He took out his knife and handed it to Mr Jarvie. 'I don't need this now,' he said simply.

To the minister it was one of the great moments of his calling. To remind him of it, that flick knife still lies on his desk — as a letter opener.     *The Friendship Book of Francis Gay, 1974*

## QUESTIONS

1. What kind of person was Mr Jarvie?
2. What does it mean to say that he had 'come up the hard way'?
3. Why do you think Mr Jarvie was so interested in the young people of the area?
4. Why did Johnny have a flick knife?
5. What did Johnny mean when he said he was at 'the cross-roads'?
6. Why did Johnny give the flick knife to Mr Jarvie?
7. Was the flick knife a sign of anything to Johnny?
8. Was the knife a sign of anything to Mr Jarvie?
9. Why does Mr Jarvie keep the knife on his desk? (List as many reasons as you can.)

This sign says 'stop' and means stop. A simple sign like this cannot *make* us stop — it can only tell us that we *should* stop.

Other signs are not so simple, and can have a powerful effect on the way we think, or act, or feel. A smile is a sign, but it does not have one simple message like the stop sign. A smile can mean 'welcome' or 'I'm happy' or it can be nasty and jeering. Seeing someone smile can have a powerful influence on us. It can make us feel happy, or welcomed, or uncomfortable. A smile is a special sign which can give different kinds of information and which can influence or affect the people who see it. This kind of sign is called a symbol.

> A symbol is a special sign which can have many meanings and which has the power to affect people.

We can say that symbols 'talk' to us in a personal way about our own lives. One symbol may say different things to different people. They can remind us of special people, places or events. A present reminds us of the person who gave it to us, what the occasion was and where we were at the time. Symbols can make us feel happy or lonely or excited. Rain beating on the window pane will make some people feel cold and miserable; others will feel happy to be indoors, snug and warm, when they hear the rain.

# EXERCISES

1. What power does the flick knife have?
2. Explain how the flick knife could be a symbol to
   (a) Johnny
   (b) Mr Jarvie.
3. Show how the following can be symbols, and how they could have powerful effects on people's feelings or actions:
   (a) the sun
   (b) a mountain
   (c) the wind
   (d) the bell at the end of the last class on Friday
   (e) a crucifix.
4. Give an example of a symbol which can affect you powerfully in the way you think, act or feel.

72

The Gospels mention several times that Jesus 'laid his hands' on people. This meant many different things at once: it meant that Jesus was going to heal the person, it meant that he cared for the person, it meant that he was not afraid of such diseases as leprosy. When Jesus laid his hands on people, they were powerfully affected: they were healed, they felt loved, they recognised that Jesus was someone special, and many became his followers. Jesus, in laying his hands on people, was therefore using a symbol.

5. Read Mark 10:13–16. In this Scripture story Jesus lays his hands on the children. Explain how this could have been a symbol for:
   (a) the children     (b) the mothers     (c) the disciples.

*Reflection*: 'You are like light for the whole world. A city built on a hill cannot be hidden. No one lights a lamp and puts it under a bowl; instead he puts it on the lampstand, where it gives light for everyone in the house. In the same way your light must shine before people, so that they will see the good things you do and praise your Father in Heaven.' Matthew 5:14–16

*Action*: Choose a symbol which represents your class community.

*Song*: 'All the Earth'

*Prayer*: Lord Jesus, you spoke to the people of your time using symbols as well as words. Help us to understand these symbols so that we can get to know you better. Amen.

# MIRACLES

## CHAPTER 23

▼

In the pictures, the cake, the cup and white dress are signs. They each represent a special time or occasion and they also tell you something about the people who made or achieved them.

## QUESTIONS

*All my own work!*

1. (a) What occasion does the cake represent?
   (b) What does the cake show about the chef?
2. (a) What occasion does the cup represent?
   (b) What does the cup which the footballer has won tell you about him?
3. (a) What occasion does the dress represent?
   (b) What does the dress she made tell you about the bride?

*I finished the dress just in time!*

*We are the champions!*

The Jewish people expected that one day God would send a saviour who would free them from their sins and set up God's Kingdom. They would know this day had arrived when they saw that the blind could see, the lame could walk, the deaf could hear, lepers were cured, the dead were raised up to life and the good news was preached to the poor.

Jesus is the Saviour who was sent by God to set up His Kingdom. His signs or miracles showed that this was happening, just as the prophets had written: He preached to the poor: Luke 6:20–26. He set captives free: Luke 5:18–26. He gave sight to the blind: Mark 8:22–25. He gave dignity to the downtrodden: Luke 7:36–50.

# EXERCISES

1. Look up each of the four references mentioned above, and read the Gospel accounts for yourself.

   The Jewish people expected God's Kingdom to be a place on this earth. Jesus had a different message. He said that the Kingdom will be among us when we are living as God wants us to live.

2. Jesus is the Son of God and everything that Jesus does tells us something about the Kingdom of God. What can we learn about God's Kingdom from the following signs?
   (a) Mark 3:1–6
   (b) Mark 4:35–41
   (c) Mark 5:21–24 and 35–43
   (d) Mark 6:30–44
   (e) Mark 8:1–9.

3. Based on what you have learned in this chapter, what do you think the Kingdom of God is like?

The miracles which Jesus worked can be called symbols because (a) they affected people powerfully and (b) they have many meanings or messages. For example, in John Chapter 9, Jesus heals a blind man:

'Jesus spat on the ground and made some mud with the spittle; he rubbed the mud on the man's eyes and said, "Go and wash your face in the Pool of Siloam." So the man went, washed his face, and came back seeing . . . "Do you believe in the Son of Man?" The man answered, "Tell me who he is, sir, so that I can believe in him." Jesus said to him, "You have already seen him, and he is the one who is talking with you now." "I believe, Lord," the man said, and knelt down before Jesus.' John 9:6–7, 35–38

*The Pool of Siloam in Jerusalem today* ▶

The man was powerfully affected; he could now see perfectly. But the miracle also helped him to see that Jesus was sent by God.

> This miracle can also be a symbol for us. It can remind us that the power of God is always there to help us in our difficulties. It shows that God will help us to understand things that are not clear to us, especially about our faith. If the miracle is a symbol for us, it will affect us powerfully, help us to believe in Jesus and go out to help others.

# QUESTIONS

Choose your favourite miracle story from the Gospel.
1. How was it a symbol for the people who actually saw the miracle happen?
2. How is it a symbol for us today?

*Reflection*: 'At once Jesus made his disciples get into the boat and go ahead of him to Bethsaida, on the other side of the lake, while he sent the crowd away. After saying goodbye to the people, he went away to a hill to pray. When evening came, the boat was in the middle of the lake, while Jesus was alone on land. He saw that his disciples were straining at the oars, because they were rowing against the wind; so some time between three and six o'clock in the morning he came to them, walking on the water. He was going to pass them by, but they saw him walking on the water. "It's a ghost!" they thought, and screamed. They were all terrified when they saw him.

'Jesus spoke to them at once. "Courage," he said. "It is I. Don't be afraid." Then he got into the boat with them, and the wind died down. The disciples were completely amazed.'
Mark 6:45–52

*Action*: Learn the hymn 'God's Spirit is in My Heart'.

*Song*: 'Glory to God, Glory'

*Prayer*: Dear Lord, we thank you for the signs of your Kingdom which are among us today. Help us to be witnesses to that Kingdom in our everyday lives. Amen.

# JESUS' DEATH AND RESURRECTION

## CHAPTER 24

Jesus' public life lasted for about three years. During that time he gained many followers but he also made many enemies. His message of repentance and love angered some people who did not think they needed any more instructions about their faith. Jesus knew that his life was in danger but he was determined to serve his father to the end.

In the gospels we are given an account of the main events which happened towards the end of Jesus' life in Palestine. Using the outline in the following pages you can act out these events in your classroom. (The outline is drawn principally from Mark 14–16 and Luke 24.)

*Characters:* Jesus; two chief priests; seven narrators; Peter; Judas; two witnesses; the High Priest; Pilate; passer-by; Salome; Mary Magdalene; angel. Everyone in the class is the 'crowd' and 'the disciples' and the 'assembly'.

*Narrator 1:* It was now two days before the feast of Passover and Unleavened Bread. The chief priests and the teachers of the law were looking for a way to arrest Jesus secretly and put him to death.

*Chief Priest 1:* We must not arrest him during the feast, or the people might riot.

*Narrator 1:* Judas Iscariot, one of the twelve disciples, went off to the chief priests in order to hand Jesus over to them. They were greatly pleased to hear what he had to say, and promised to give him money. So Judas started looking for a good chance to betray Jesus.

**Narrator 2:** On the first day of the feast of Unleavened Bread, the day the lambs for the Passover meal were killed, the disciples prepared the meal. While they were at table eating, Jesus said to his twelve disciples:

**Jesus:** I tell you this: one of you will betray me — one who is eating with me.

**Disciples:** Surely you don't mean me, do you?

**Jesus:** It will be one of you twelve, one who dips his bread in the dish with me. The Son of Man will die as the Scriptures say he will; but how terrible for that man who will betray the Son of Man! It would have been better for that man if he had never been born!

**Narrator 2:** While they were eating, Jesus took the bread, gave a prayer of thanks, broke it, and gave it to his disciples.

**Jesus:** Take it, this is my body.

**Narrator 2:** Then he took the cup filled with wine, gave thanks to God, and handed it to them; and they all drank from it.

**Jesus:** This is my blood which is poured out for many, for the forgiveness of sins. Do this in memory of me.

**Narrator 2:** Then they sang a hymn and went out to the Mount of Olives.

**Jesus:** All of you will run away and leave me, because the Scripture says, 'God will kill the shepherd and the sheep will all be scattered.' But after I am raised to life I will go to Galilee ahead of you.

**Peter:** I will never leave you, even though all the rest do!

**Jesus:** Remember this! Before the cock crows two times tonight, you will say three times that you do not know me.

| Peter: | I will never say I do not know you, even if I have to die with you. |
|---|---|
| Disciples: | We will never deny you either. |
| Narrator 3: | They came to a place called Gethsemane. |
| Jesus: | All of you sit here while I pray. Peter, James and John, come with me. |
| Narrator 3: | Distress and anguish came over Jesus. |
| Jesus: | The sorrow in my heart is so great that it almost crushes me. Stay here and watch. |
| Narrator 3: | Jesus went a little farther on, threw himself on the ground and prayed. |
| Jesus: | Father! My Father! All things are possible for you. Take this cup away from me. But not what I want, but what you want. |
| Narrator 3: | Jesus returned and found the three disciples asleep. |
| Jesus: | Simon, are you asleep? Weren't you able to stay awake for one hour? |
| Narrator 3: | Jesus returned a second and a third time and found the three still asleep. |
| Jesus: | Are you still sleeping and resting? Enough! The hour has come! Look, the Son of Man is now handed over to the power of sinful men. Get up, let us go. Look, here is the man who is betraying me! |
| Narrator 3: | Judas arrived with a crowd carrying swords and clubs, sent by the chief priests, the teachers of the law and the elders. |
| Judas: | The man I kiss is the one you want. Arrest him and take him away under guard. |
| Narrator 3: | Judas kissed Jesus, then the soldiers arrested Jesus and put him under guard. After some disturbance Jesus was led away and all the disciples fled. |

**Narrator 4:** Jesus was brought before the assembly of the High Priest. They tried to find some evidence against Jesus in order to put him to death; but they could find none.

**Witness 1:** I heard him say, 'I will tear down this temple which men made, and after three days I will build one that is not made by men.'

**Witness 2:** I heard him say he would rebuild it in two days.

**High Priest:** Have you no answer to the accusation they bring against you?

**Narrator 4:** Jesus kept quiet and would not say a word.

**High Priest:** Are you the Messiah, the Son of the Blessed God?

**Jesus:** I am, and you will all see the Son of Man seated at the right side of the Almighty, and coming with the clouds of heaven!

**High Priest:** Enough! We don't need any more witnesses! You heard his wicked words. What is your decision?

**Assembly:** Guilty! Guilty! Let him be put to death.

**Narrator 4:** They took Jesus and put him in chains and handed him over to Pilate — the Roman governor, who alone had the power to put Jesus to death. Meanwhile, Peter had already claimed three times that he did not even know Jesus.

**Pilate:** Are you the king of the Jews?

**Jesus:** So you say.

**Narrator 5:** Pilate continued to question Jesus and was very surprised that Jesus refused to answer. Pilate went out and asked the crowds should he free Barab'bas, a murderer, or Jesus, since it was the custom at Passover to free one prisoner.

**Crowd:** We want Barab'bas! We want Barab'bas!

| | |
|---|---|
| *Pilate:* | What, then, do you want me to do with the one you call the King of the Jews? |
| *Crowd:* | Nail him to the cross! |
| *Pilate:* | But what crime has he committed? |
| *Crowd:* | Nail him to the cross! |
| *Narrator 5:* | Pilate wanted to please the crowd, so he set Barab'bas free for them. Then he had Jesus whipped and handed him over to be nailed to the cross. They brought Jesus to a place called 'Golgotha'. Here they nailed him to the cross at nine o'clock in the morning. They divided his clothes among themselves. People passing by shook their heads and hurled insults at Jesus. |
| *Passer-by:* | Aha! You were going to tear down the temple and build it up in three days! Now come down from the cross and save yourself! |
| *Chief Priest 2:* | He saved others, but he cannot save himself! Let us see the Messiah, the King of Israel, come down from the cross now and we will believe in him! |
| *Narrator 5:* | At three o'clock, with a loud cry, Jesus died. |
| *Narrator 6:* | Joseph of Arimathea went to Pilate and asked him for the body of Jesus. Pilate first made sure that Jesus was really dead and then agreed to hand over the body. Joseph brought a linen sheet, took the body down, wrapped it in the sheet and placed it in a grave which had been dug out of the rock. Then he rolled a large stone across the entrance to the grave. Mary Magdalene and another Mary were watching and saw where Jesus was placed.

Very early on Sunday morning, Mary Magdalene and two other women bought spices to go and anoint the body of Jesus. |
| *Mary Magdalene:* | Joseph used a very large stone. Who will roll it away for us from the entrance to the grave? |

*Salome:* Look! The stone has already been rolled back!

*Narrator 6:* They entered the grave where they saw a young man sitting at the right, wearing a white robe, and they were filled with alarm.

*Angel:* Don't be alarmed. I know you are looking for Jesus of Nazareth, who was nailed to the cross. He is not here — he has been raised! Look, here is the spot where they placed him. Now go and give this message to his disciples, including Peter: 'He is going to Galilee ahead of you; there will you see him, just as he told you.'

*Narrator 6:* The women told the disciples that Jesus had risen, but the apostles would not believe them. Peter got up and ran to the grave; he bent down and saw the grave clothes and nothing else. Then he went home wondering at what had happened.

*Narrator 7:* After Jesus rose from death he appeared first to Mary Magdalene. After this he appeared in a different manner to two of the disciples while they were on their way to Emmaus. Last of all Jesus appeared to the eleven apostles.

| | |
|---|---|
| *Jesus:* | Peace be with you. |
| *Disciples:* | It is a ghost! |
| *Jesus:* | Why are you afraid? Look at my hands and my feet and see that it is I, myself. |
| *Narrator 7:* | They still could not believe, they were so full of joy and wonder; so he asked them: |
| *Jesus:* | Do you have anything to eat here? |
| *Narrator 7:* | They gave him a piece of cooked fish which he ate in front of them. |
| *Jesus:* | This is what is written in the Scriptures. The Messiah must suffer, and rise from death on the third day. In his name the message about repentance and the forgiveness of sins must be preached to all nations beginning in Jerusalem. You are witnesses of all these things. |
| *Narrator 7:* | Many days later Jesus led his disciples out of the city as far as Bethany, where he raised his hands and blessed them. As he was blessing them, he departed from them and was taken up into heaven. They worshipped him and went back into Jerusalem, filled with great joy, and spent all their time in the temple giving thanks to God. |

**Some terms used in this chapter**

*Passover/Feast of Unleavened Bread:* a Jewish feast celebrating the flight from Egypt.

*Son of Man:* a term from the Old Testament used to describe the Messiah.

*Chief Priests, teachers of the law and elders* were different leaders in the Jewish community.

*The Assembly of the High Priest* was the ruling group of the Jewish community.

# QUESTIONS

1. What are your feelings about this story?
2. How did the followers of Jesus feel when Jesus was taken from the Garden of Gethsemane?
3. How do you think Jesus felt at this time?
4. Did Jesus' followers feel differently after the resurrection?
5. What, in your opinion, is the most important moment in this Gospel account? Explain why.
6. What is the meaning or message of these events for you?

The people followed Jesus because they believed in him and in his message. They saw signs of his power in his miracles. Jesus taught them how to live as children of God, through his parables and especially by the way he himself lived. He said that those who wanted to be in his community would have to deny themselves as he did and take up their cross to follow him. Throughout his life Jesus always chose the loving action instead of the self-centred one. When he was tired or hungry he would often keep going because the people needed him. We are asked to deny ourselves in the same way; to do the loving action, even if it is difficult.

Jesus knew that he was facing death if he continued with his work, but again he kept going. His death seemed like the end of everything for his followers. Instead he was resurrected and appeared among them. He promised that for his followers death was no longer the end, but the beginning of everlasting life.

For us this means that any time we 'die' to ourselves we are learning to be more loving. In this way our lives will be really worth while and not be selfishly wasted.

# EXERCISES

1. What can we learn about life and death from Jesus' life, death and resurrection?
2. Describe one example to show how denying yourself can make you a better person. For example, if a shop assistant gives you too much change you could keep it and buy something you wanted. If you decide to deny yourself and return the money, you are training yourself to be an honest person.

*Reflection:* 'Then Jesus called the crowd and his disciples to him. "If anyone wants to come with me," he told them, "he must forget himself, carry his cross, and follow me. For whoever wants to save his own life will lose it; but whoever loses his life for me and for the Gospel will save it. Does a person gain anything if he wins the whole world but loses his life? Of course not! There is nothing he can give to regain his life."' Mark 8:34–37

*Action:* Watch out for stories in the newspaper or on television that are examples of people who denied themselves and were changed for the better by this experience.

*Song:* 'Be Not Afraid'

*Prayer:* Lord Jesus, by your life, death and resurrection you have shown us that death leads to life. Give us the courage to be able to die to our selfishness and live for love. Amen.

# UNIT V

## THE SACRAMENTS

# SACRAMENTS

## CHAPTER 25

▼

On my way to school, I used to see this man at the corner of Duke Street and Poplar Road. He sat on a bit of a low wall and used a blue plastic lunch-box as a begging bowl. Sometimes he was drunk and shouted at the passers-by. Most people — including me — tried to ignore him, and pretend he wasn't there. Some people even crossed the road so that they didn't have to go past him. One day as I was going by he was lying on the pavement in beside the wall, fast asleep and snoring, using the lunch-box for a pillow. It looked very funny, but also a bit sad. While I was looking at him I suddenly thought, God thinks that this man is as important as the Pope. Imagine — God loves him as much as he loves Mother Theresa of Calcutta. It gave me a weird feeling — as if God was very close to me, looking through my eyes at the man. I realised then that I couldn't keep on ignoring the man day after day. Even though I couldn't *do* anything for him, I could at least say hello.

## *Q* UESTIONS

1. How did the student think and feel about the man at first?
2. What made the student realise that God was near?
3. What difference did it make to the student, knowing that God was present?

Most of us think about God some of the time, for instance when we are praying or passing a church. Occasionally something happens that makes us realise just how close God is to us, even when we are not thinking of Him at all. For example, if someone gives us a much-needed helping hand, or we happen to be caught in a magnificent thunderstorm, we may notice God's loving, powerful presence. The student in the story realised that God was near when she stopped and really looked at the man in the street. God doesn't force Himself on us, but He does give us many opportunities to meet Him in this way. Each time this happens we have the chance to improve our friendship with God. Usually we change a little as a result, and become more loving towards God and other people.

# EXERCISES

1. Can you remember a time when you really noticed that God was near to you? Explain.
2. If this has happened to you, did it affect the way you thought or acted at the time? Explain.

It is easy to miss meeting God, unless we are really looking out for Him. However, the Church gives us special opportunities, when we can be certain of meeting God if we want to meet him. These special occasions are called sacraments — Baptism, Confirmation, Eucharist, Reconciliation, Anointing of the Sick, Matrimony and Holy Orders. Because of these sacraments, we can be certain of receiving God's blessing and help at all the most important times in our lives. The sacraments also give us an opportunity to praise and thank God for all His love and care. *Sacraments are special opportunities for meeting God.* In each of the sacraments, God speaks to us through signs and symbols. When we meet God in this way we are powerfully affected, both as individuals and as a community.

3.  Examine each of the following seven situations:
    (a) Growing up and becoming mature
    (b) Daily life in the community
    (c) Priesthood
    (d) Married love and family life
    (e) Being born into the community
    (f) Being sick in body or mind
    (g) Being forgiven and forgiving.
Which of the sacraments would be most needed at each of these times? Explain.
4.  Look up each of the following Scripture references. Write down which of the sacraments you are reminded of as you read each passage:
    (a) John 6:53–58
    (b) Mark 3:13–15
    (c) Matthew 28:16–20
    (d) Luke 7:36–50
    (e) Matthew 19:4–6
    (f) Mark 8:22–26
    (g) Acts 8:14–17

*Reflection*: 'Out of the fullness of his grace he has blessed us all, giving us one blessing after another . . . grace and truth came through Jesus Christ. No one has ever seen God. The only Son, who is the same as God and is at the Father's side, he has made Him known.' John 1:16, 17b, 18

*Action*: Choose a day when you will make a special effort to meet God. For example, you might go for a walk and allow the things you see to remind you of God; or you might remember that all the people you meet are loved by God and try to treat them as well as you can.

*Song*: 'Be Still and Know I Am God'

*Prayer*: Lord Jesus, we thank you for the opportunities you give us to meet with God. Help us to notice how near God is to us at all times. Amen.

### Some Information

A *ceremony* or *rite* is the name given to the special words, actions and signs which are used to help us to celebrate the sacraments.

In each sacrament the priest acts on behalf of Jesus. The priest is called the *celebrant*.

The celebrant wears special clothes to show that the sacrament is a Special Occasion.

The **alb** is a long white robe.

The **stole** is a long garment worn around the neck.

The **cincture** is a rope belt.

The **chasuble** is a large garment
which can be highly decorated.

The **surplice** is a large-sleeved,
half-length white garment.

The **cassock** is a long black garment.

# BAPTISM

## CHAPTER 26

▼

Nweke was born in a small village in Eastern Nigeria. When he was twenty-eight days old, the time came for the Asa Nwa ceremony, when he would be named and presented to all the people in his village. His parents brought him to the Senior Man of their Umunna (a quarter of the village) for the occasion.

The baby was held up and shown to the people, who all cheered loudly to welcome him into the community. The Senior Man then asked what names the child was to be given. His mother, father, relations and neighbours all gave him names, and these were called out to the people. (Although he was given many names, his mother liked the name 'Nweke' best, so afterwards that was what he was usually called.)

After the naming ceremony, the Senior Man took out a hoe and a machete and showed them to the baby, saying, 'My son, with these farm implements your father lived well. We call on you to acquaint yourself with them properly and be hard-working. We wish you good fruits of your labour. Live, grow and wax strong.'

After this speech there was feasting and celebrating: Nweke was now a real member of the village community.

adapted from *A Nigerian Villager in Two Worlds*
by Dilin Okafor-Omali

## EXERCISES

1. Why was the Asa Nwa ceremony important to the people of the village?
2. Even though Nweke was too young to know what was happening, was the ceremony in any way important to him?
3. Nweke was given names by many people. Was this a sign of anything?
4. Were the hoe and machete signs? Explain.
5. Were the hoe and machete symbols? Explain.

All over the world, people celebrate new beginnings: New Year's Eve, moving to a new home, getting a job, or joining an organisation like the Girl Guides or Boy Scouts. Sometimes they use a ceremony or rite. Most celebrations include signs of what the new life of the person will be like. In the Asa Nwa ceremony, the hoe and machete are signs that Nweke is now part of a farming community and that one day his community will teach Nweke how to grow his own food using a hoe and machete.

A new baby in the family is a special new beginning, because it is the start of a new life for the baby and for the family. Like Nweke's community, many people celebrate the birth of a baby with both a ceremony and a party.

6.  Have you ever celebrated a new beginning? Describe the occasion.
7.  Were any signs used in the celebration? Explain.
8.  How is the birth of a baby a new beginning for the family?

When someone accepts Jesus' invitation to join the Christian community, this is a new beginning for the person and for the community. We say that the person is 'born' into a new life. The new Christian hopes to follow God's plan for love and happiness and the community promises to help. *The Sacrament of Baptism is the celebration in which the community of faith invites us to meet God in a special way and become part of His Christian family.* The celebration is a special rite or ceremony, which usually takes place in church.

When a baby is baptised he/she does not know what is happening, but as a baby grows he/she begins to learn from the community the gift that Baptism is. As well as his/her parents, the baby has two godparents or sponsors who promise to help to teach the child about the faith. The young person gradually realises that God has welcomed him/her into His community as a sign of His love.

9.  Can you think of any things which you do because you are baptised into the Community of Faith?
10. Can you remember how you learned that you were baptised and that God loved you? Share your memories with the class.
11. Bring in photographs of your Baptism. Find your baptismal certificate.

The Rite of Baptism uses many signs which show what the life of the new Christian will be like from now on.

Baptising with *water:* This is a sign of the beginning of new life; the ending of an old way of life; being cleansed.

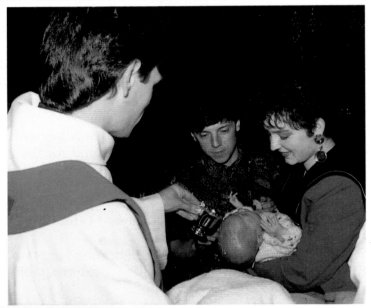

Baptising with *oil* (chrism): This is a sign of being strong; being healed; that you are now a follower of Christ, the 'anointed' One.

Receiving the *light* of Christ: This is a sign that Jesus is with you; you will be a light to others; you will love other people.

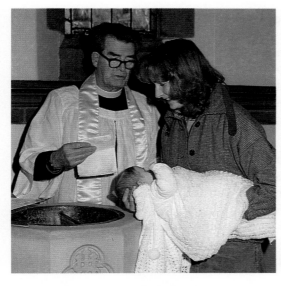

Being dressed in a *white garment:* This is a sign of your new life with the Risen Jesus and that you will try not to sin.

These are not just ordinary signs. They are special symbols because they have many meanings and actually change the person who is being baptised.

# EXERCISES

1. Find out all you can about water, how it is used, where it can be found, why it is necessary for life, how it can be dangerous and so on. Explain why water is a good symbol for Baptism.

2. Find out all you can about oil and light, their uses, where you will find them and why they are needed. Explain why they are good symbols for Baptism.

*Reflection*: 'I will sprinkle clean water on you and make you clean from all your idols . . . I will give you a new heart and a new mind.' (Ezekiel 36:25a, 26a)

*Action*: Find out about Baptisms in your parish church. If possible, attend a Baptism. Perhaps you could arrange to decorate the church with posters for the occasion.

*Song*: 'The Light of Christ'

*Prayer*: Lord Jesus, we thank you for the gift of Baptism. May our words and actions show your love to the world. Amen.

### Outline of the Rite of Baptism for a Child

*Introduction to the Rite*

1.  The celebrant says a few words to welcome everyone.
2.  The parents ask for their child to be baptised into the Christian community.
3.  The celebrant reminds the parents that it will be their duty to bring up their child in the Christian faith, when the child is baptised.

*Celebration of God's Word in Scripture*

1.  The congregation listens to a passage from the Old or New Testament. For example, Matthew 28:18–20, Romans 6:3–5 or Galatians 3:26–28.
2.  The celebrant reminds everyone what Baptism means.
3.  Everyone prays the Prayers of the Faithful.
4.  The celebrant anoints the child with oil and prays for him/her.

*Celebration of the Sacrament of Baptism*

1.  The celebrant blesses the water.
2.  The parents and godparents speak for the child and promise that he/she rejects everything evil and believes in God the Father, the Son and the Holy Spirit.
3.  The celebrant pours the water over the child's head, saying: 'I baptise you in the name of the Father, and of the Son and of the Holy Spirit.'
4.  The celebrant anoints the child's head with chrism.
5.  The parents have a white garment for the newly baptised child to wear. The celebrant says: 'See in this white garment the outward sign of your Christian dignity.'
6.  The parents hold the baptismal candle for their child as the celebrant says: 'Receive the light of Christ.'
7.  The celebrant touches and prays over the child's ears and mouth: 'The Lord Jesus made the deaf hear and the dumb speak. May he soon touch your ears to receive his word, and your mouth to proclaim his faith, to the praise and glory of God the Father.'

*Conclusion of the Rite*

1.  The celebrant prays: 'Dearly beloved, this child has been reborn in Baptism. He/she is now called the child of God, for so indeed he/she is. In Confirmation he/she will receive the fullness of God's Spirit. In Holy Communion he/she will share the banquet of Christ's sacrifice, calling God his/her Father in the midst of the church.'
2.  Everyone prays the Our Father.
3.  The celebrant blesses the child's mother, then the father, and then all who are present.

# EUCHARIST

## CHAPTER 27

Suppose it is your birthday next week. Your parents tell you that they will give you £5 and you can do one of two things:

(a)  Invite ten of your friends around to your home to listen to records and have lemonade and crisps, or whatever snacks you can afford with £5;

(b)  Spend the money on your own favourite foods, sweets or soft drinks, and eat them yourself in the bedroom, alone, listening to records, or reading or whatever you like.

These are your *only* choices. Which would you choose and why? Try to decide as a class which would be the better choice.

Many of us like to celebrate our birthday by having a meal with other people, even if it is only lemonade and crisps. In fact, we celebrate almost every important event in our lives by eating and drinking — think of Christmas, or a wedding.

Like most other important celebrations, a birthday is a time for being happy, remembering and looking forward:

*Being happy* — to enjoy a special occasion with family and friends.

*Remembering* — the day we were born, the past year.

*Looking forward* — to the coming year, to the rest of our lives.

## QUESTIONS

1.  Can you think of any occasions in our lives which we celebrate with a meal?
2.  Choose two of your examples and in each case explain
    (a) what is being remembered
    (b) to what are the people looking forward
    (c) what else is making the people happy at the celebration.
3.  Why is a meal such a good way to celebrate with other people?

Every day, as members of the Christian community, we try to follow God's plan which Jesus teaches us. God is always with us, giving us the power to love, to help, to forgive and to pray. Jesus wanted us to be able to celebrate this. Therefore he gives us a special opportunity to meet God and become a more loving and united community. The celebration is called the Sacrament of the Eucharist, or the Mass. The Eucharist is celebrated with a ceremony or rite which includes readings from Scripture, special prayers, and most importantly, a sacred meal. At Mass the Risen Lord gives himself to the Father and to us. When we come together to celebrate Mass or the Eucharist, we remember that Jesus is risen and that he is with us. We know that he continues to give all his love to the Father as he did during his life and on the cross. We give ourselves and our love to the Father with the Lord Jesus.

The first Eucharist was celebrated by Jesus with his disciples at the Last Supper.

'While they were eating, Jesus took a piece of bread, gave a prayer of thanks, broke (the bread) and gave it to his disciples. "Take (this) and eat it," he said, "This is my body." Then he took a cup (filled with wine) gave thanks to God, and gave it to them. "Drink it, all of you," he said, "This is my blood poured out for many for the forgiveness of sins. Do this in memory of me." Matthew 26:26–28, Luke 22:19

When we celebrate the Eucharist:

*We remember* God's goodness to us and especially that He sent Jesus to us.

*We look forward* to our future together, as a community growing closer to God and to each other; and we look forward to the kingdom promised to us by Jesus.

*We are happy* to be together praising and thanking God.

# EXERCISES

1. Mention some things in your life and in the life of your community which you could remember and thank God for in the Eucharist. (For example: gifts or talents, relationships, natural surroundings or other blessings)
2. How could the Eucharist help your community to grow closer together and closer to God?
3. When you are celebrating the Eucharist, how could you show that you understand the importance of what is happening?

The Eucharistic rite uses many special symbols to show what it is like to be in a Christian community loved by God.

*We eat the Bread of Life, the Body of Jesus*: This is a symbol of the life that God gives us; of our unity with Jesus; of our unity with each other.

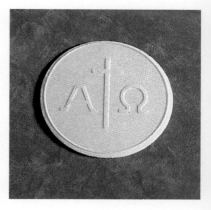

*Sometimes we share the cup*: This is a symbol both of the suffering of Jesus and the joy we experience as children of God.

*We share a special meal together*: This is a symbol of friendship in the community; of unity in the community; of God's generosity to us.

These special symbols have many meanings and have the power to change the community through the sacrament of the Eucharist. They make the community more united. They make us feel happy because we are loved by God.

# EXERCISES

1. Why is a meal a good symbol to use in the Eucharistic celebration?
2. Choose one of the topics 'bread' or 'wine'. Prepare a poster, drawing or project on your topic, showing the value and importance it has all over the world. For example, bread is an important food, it is made up of many grains of wheat and so on. Explain why bread (or wine) is a good symbol to use in the Eucharist.

*Reflection*: 'Jesus said to them, "I am telling you the truth: if you do not eat the flesh of the Son of Man and drink his blood, you will not have life in yourselves. Whoever eats my flesh and drinks my blood has eternal life, and I will raise him to life on the last day."' John 6:53–54

*Action*: Decide to listen carefully during the next Eucharist you take part in and choose one idea which you will put into practice in your life.

*Song*: 'I Am the Bread of Life'

*Prayer*: Lord, we know that you love us because you give us yourself in the Eucharist. Help us to give ourselves to others by serving them. Amen.

**Outline of the Celebration of the Eucharist**

*Introduction*

1. Entrance and entrance song.
2. The penitential rite.
3. The Gloria, a hymn of praise to God.
4. Opening prayer.

*Celebration of God's Word in Scripture*

1. First reading (usually from the Old Testament).
2. Responsorial psalm.
3. Second reading (from the New Testament).
4. The Gospel acclamation (a cry of praise to God).
5. The Gospel reading.
6. The homily (a short talk linking the Gospel to our everyday lives).
7. The creed (a statement of what we believe).
8. The prayers of the faithful/bidding prayers.

*Celebration of the Eucharist*

1. Offertory procession/presentation of the gifts.
2. The celebrant accepts the gifts at the altar.
3. The celebrant prays privately and washes his hands.
4. The celebrant says the prayers over the gifts.
5. The Eucharistic prayer
   (a) This starts with a dialogue between the celebrant and the people:
   *Celebrant:* The Lord be with you.
   *People:* And also with you.
   *Celebrant:* Lift up your hearts.
   *People:* We have raised them up to the Lord.
   *Celebrant:* Let us give thanks to the Lord our God.
   *People:* It is right to give Him thanks and praise.
   (b) The preface is a prayer of praise and thanks to God the Father.
   (c) Everyone sings or says the Holy, Holy, Holy acclamation.
   (d) There is a prayer to the Holy Spirit.
   (e) At the Consecration, we recall the Last Supper, and Jesus' death on the cross. The bread and wine become the body and blood of Jesus.
   (f) The people sing or say the memorial acclamation. For example: 'Christ has died, Christ has risen, Christ will come again.'
   (g) There is another prayer to the Holy Spirit.

(h) There are prayers of petition or intercession for the Church, for Christian unity, for the dead and for us to be united with the saints.

(i) The Eucharistic prayer ends with a doxology, a special prayer of thanks and praise to God:
*Celebrant:* Through him (Jesus), with him, and in him, in the unity of the Holy Spirit, all glory and honour is yours, Almighty Father, for ever and ever.
*People:* Amen.

6.  Communion Rite
    (a) Everyone prays the Our Father.
    (b) There is a prayer for peace.
    (c) We offer a sign of peace to each other.
    (d) The breaking of bread: the people sing or say the 'Lamb of God', while the priest breaks the host.
    (e) The people pray: 'Lord I am not worthy that you should come to me, but only say the word, and I shall be healed.'
    (f) The people receive Holy Communion.
    (g) The people thank God by praying privately and by singing.
    (h) The prayer after communion is the official prayer of thanks to God.

7.  Conclusion
    (a) The celebrant blesses the people and says, 'Go in peace to love and serve the Lord.' The people reply, 'Thanks be to God.'
    (b) A concluding hymn may be sung.

# CONFIRMATION

## CHAPTER 28

One of the big complaints that young people sometimes have is that they are 'treated like kids' and given no freedom. Their parents and teachers sometimes complain that young people act like three-year-olds and cannot be trusted! Use the following questionnaire to get an idea of just how grown-up or mature you are.

In your copy, put a circle around the answer which applies to you. For example: Are you a student? Yes. No. Sometimes. (Put Yes in your copy.)

1. If you are asked to do something at home, do you usually do it?
   Yes. No. Sometimes.
2. Do you ever offer to help at home, before being asked?
   Yes. No. Sometimes.
3. Do you make sure to leave enough time to get all your homework done?
   Yes. No. Sometimes.
4. If you have a row with a friend, are you willing to be the first to make up?
   Yes. No. Sometimes.
5. Do you try to be on time for Mass and pay attention when you are there?
   Yes. No. Sometimes.
6. When something makes you angry, can you control your temper?
   Yes. No. Sometimes.
7. Do you try to help people who are less well-off than yourself.
   Yes. No. Sometimes.

In your copy, put a box around the answer which applies to you. For example: Are you under two years old? Yes. No. Sometimes. (Put No in your copy.)

1. Do you find yourself doing things you feel you shouldn't do, just to go along with the 'gang'?
   Yes. No. Sometimes.

2.  Do you join in bullying or jeering at others?
    (Yes.) No. Sometimes.
3.  Do you lie to get out of awkward situations?
    Yes. (No.) Sometimes.
4.  Do you show off when members of the opposite sex are
    present?
    Yes. (No.) Sometimes.
5.  Do you sulk when you don't get your own way?
    Yes. (No.) Sometimes.
6.  Do you rattle off your prayers without thinking of what
    you are saying?
    Yes. No. (Sometimes.)
7.  Do you throw litter on the ground instead of using the bin?
    (Yes.) No. Sometimes.

Mark yourself in the following way:
For every 'yes' you have *circled*, give yourself **4** points.
For every 'yes' you have put in a *box*, give yourself **0** points.
For every 'no' you have *circled*, give yourself **0** points.
For every 'no' you have put in a *box*, give yourself **4** points.
For every 'sometimes' you have *circled*, give yourself **2** points.
For every 'sometimes' you have put in a *box*, give yourself **1** point.
Now add up your points!

*0–14 points:*   You seem to be a bit immature. Did you mark
yourself too hard, or perhaps you have never realised that
growing up means giving up childish ways?

*15–28 points:*  You are quite mature in many ways, but still
have some distance to go. Remember, people don't suddenly
become mature: we have to work at it.

*29–42 points:*  This is a very good score. You are not perfect, but
you are well on the way to being a really mature person. Keep
up the good work!

*43–56 points:*  You seem almost too good to be true! You are
indeed a very mature person for your age, or indeed for any
age. (You were honest with yourself, weren't you?)

Growing up means more freedom. It also means taking more
responsibility for what we do. Other people used to make all
our decisions for us; now we are faced with making up our
own minds. We have to choose what friends to have, what to
wear, which sport to concentrate on, which subjects to study in
school, or even what to do when someone annoys us.

Throughout our lives we constantly face new choices and we
don't always feel ready for them. The support and advice of
other people helps, but we do need to think things out for
ourselves and be able to make a wise decision.

# QUESTIONS

1. What new choices have you made in the last year?
2. What kind of decisions do you find the hardest to make?

As Christians, all of our decisions should be loving and unselfish. God gives us His Holy Spirit to help and guide us as we make our choices. When young people are faced with new challenges, the Spirit of God is always with them. In the Sacrament of Confirmation we celebrate the fact that the Spirit is in us. Through this sacrament, we meet God in a special way as He blesses us with the gifts of the Holy Spirit. This sacrament is called 'Confirmation' because it confirms that we are part of the Christian family. The gifts of the Holy Spirit give us the strength to be fully committed members of the Church; they help us to make wise decisions, and to have the courage to stand up for what is right.

# EXERCISES

1. Are there any situations in your life in which you need the special guidance of the Holy Spirit? Explain.
2. Look back over the situations mentioned in the questionnaire at the beginning of this chapter. Try to work out what a Christian would do in each situation, when guided by the Holy Spirit.
3. What symbols are used in the Sacrament of Confirmation? (You may need to check the rite at the end of the chapter.) Draw and describe the symbols in words, and explain what they mean and what they do.

*Reflection*: 'Jesus said, "If you love me, you will obey my commandments. I will ask the Father, and He will give you another Helper, the Spirit of truth, to stay with you forever."' John 14:15–16

*Action*: Decide to ask the Holy Spirit for guidance and help first thing every day. You might like to use the prayer on this page.

*Song*: 'Spirit of the Living God'

*Prayer*: Come, Holy Spirit, and fill our hearts with your love. May your love in us be seen in all our thoughts, words and actions. Amen.

**Outline of the Rite of Confirmation**

The Sacrament of Confirmation is usually celebrated during a celebration of the Eucharist.

*Introduction*
1.   The Mass begins in the usual way. The people and the celebrant greet each other, there is a short Rite of Reconciliation, and the opening prayers of the Eucharist are said.

*Celebration of God's Word in Scripture*
1.   Everyone listens to the readings, which help them to think about the meaning of Confirmation. For example: first reading, Ezekiel 36:24–28; second reading, Acts 8:1, 4, 14–17.
2.   The bishop gives a homily about Confirmation.
3.   Everyone renews the promises which they made (or which were made for them) at Baptism.

*The Laying on of Hands*

The bishop places his hands on the head of each candidate and prays for the Holy Spirit to live in him/her in a special way. All of the people join in his prayer by saying 'Amen' at the end.

The people who are going to be confirmed (the candidates) go to the sanctuary with their sponsors.

*The Anointing with Chrism*
1.   Each candidate kneels in front of the bishop.
2.   Using his thumb, the bishop makes the Sign of the Cross on the candidate's forehead and says: '(Name) be sealed with the gift of the Holy Spirit.'

*Prayers of the Faithful*
Everyone prays the prayers of the faithful.

*Celebration of the Eucharist*
The Mass continues as usual, starting with the offertory.

# RECONCILIATION

## CHAPTER 29
▼

Damien called the meeting to order. Everyone on the committee was instantly quiet and looked eagerly at their chairman. He turned to the treasurer: 'Helen, have we reached our target?' Helen opened the bank book and replied, 'We now have £29 over the target.' Everyone clapped and cheered excitedly. All the hard work of fund-raising had been worth it. At last they could have enough money to build and run their own skate-board club. It was going to be great fun . . .

'Hello. 110927.'

'Hello. Is Mr O'Connor there?'

'Yes, speaking.'

'Oh, good. This is Jo Delaney. Have you heard about the new skate-board club that is being planned?'

'Yes, indeed I have. I believe they have enough money now to go ahead with the project.'

'Well, that's the problem. They want to build the track in that field beside Clancy's.'

'But . . . that's beside our estate!'

'Exactly. Can't you just imagine it? Kids will be there at all hours of the day and night, shouting and roaring, throwing litter and bottles everywhere. Of course they *say* it will be properly organised, but it only takes one or two bad apples to ruin the whole barrel.'

'I'm afraid you are right, Mrs Delaney. Most of these youngsters are great kids, but it's the rowdy ones who will cause the trouble.'

'They say of course that no alcohol will be allowed on the premises, but what's to stop them drinking *off* the premises, or on our streets in front of our young children?'

'I'm sure the committee will see reason when we explain to them that they will have to build their track somewhere else. Perhaps we could get representatives of the Residents' Association to talk to them . . .'

## Skate-board Club Row

Reporter J. O'Neill

Talks between the Cairnfield Residents' Association and the skate-board club committee broke down yesterday. Angry words were spoken on both sides over the siting of the proposed skate-board club. The committee says that it is determined to go ahead as planned. Chairman Damien Smith said that there wasn't another suitable site in the locality. 'There's no point in having a skate-board club five miles away,' he stated.

The Residents say they will picket the field and organise protests to make sure that the work does not go ahead. Mrs Delaney told this reporter, 'We are entitled to peace and security. It's all very well saying that there will be no trouble, but they could be having cider parties and be joy-riding down our streets within the year.' Is there any hope that a solution will be found to this difficult problem?

# QUESTIONS

1. Explain in your own words what is the real problem in this situation.
2. What will have to happen if the problem is to be solved?
3. List as many different 'solutions' to the problem as you can. Put this list on the blackboard or on a flip-chart. As a class, decide
   (a) What are the advantages of each 'solution'?
   (b) What are the disadvantages of each 'solution'?
4. Work out which is the best solution overall for this situation.

Our relationships with each other can be damaged or even destroyed when we refuse to be loving. This can happen because we don't want to know about what other people need. It can happen when we don't bother to be kind, or patient or understanding. It is not easy to repair a relationship that has broken down. All Christians, however, are responsible for building up good relationships in the community, because Jesus said, 'Love one another.' With the help of the Holy Spirit, Christians are able to be sorry for being unloving and are able to forgive each other. In this way we are reconciled with one another, and can be happy again.

5. What can make it difficult for us to become reconciled with each other after a row?
6. 'But I'm in the right. He's the one who picked a row with me. There is nothing I can do.' What advice would you give this person, as a Christian?

When we sin against each other, we also sin against God, who loves each one of us. When we become reconciled with each other, we also need to become reconciled with God, who is ready to forgive us at any time. In the Sacrament of Reconciliation or penance we have a special opportunity to meet with God, tell Him we are sorry and receive His forgiveness. This sacrament is also a way to celebrate all the reconciliations which happen in the community.

# EXERCISES

1. What do you find helpful about the Sacrament of Reconciliation?
2. What do you find difficult?
3. What symbols are used in the Rite of Reconciliation? (You might need to check the last page of this chapter.) Draw or describe the symbols in words and explain what they mean and what they do.

*Reflection*: 'So then, confess your sins to one another and pray for one another, so that you will be healed. The prayer of a good person has a powerful effect.'  James 5:16

*Action*: If there is anyone with whom you are on bad terms at the moment, decide to become reconciled with him/her as soon as you can. Be determined to make the first move.

*Song*: 'Lay Your Hands'

*Prayer*: Lord, forgive us our sins as we forgive those who sin against us.  Amen.

## Outline of the Rite of Reconciliation for One Person

### Introduction

1. The priest welcomes the penitent.
2. The penitent makes the Sign of the Cross.
3. The priest encourages the penitent to trust in God.

### Celebration of the Word of God (optional)

The priest reads a passage from Scripture which speaks about God's mercy and the need to change from evil to good in our lives. For example: Matthew 6:14–15; Mark 1:14–15; Luke 6:31–38; Romans 5:8–9.

### Confession of Sin

The priest helps the penitent to make a good confession. He encourages the penitent to be truly sorry. He gives the penitent a 'penance', a prayer or action which helps the penitent to try to make up for the damage his/her sins have caused.

### Act of Sorrow

The penitent tells God that he/she is truly sorry for sinning, and promises not to sin again.

### Absolution

The priest puts his hands over the penitent's head (or holds out his right hand) and says:

> 'God, the Father of mercies,
> through the death and resurrection of His Son
> has reconciled the world to Himself
> and sent the Holy Spirit among us
> for the forgiveness of sins;
> through the ministry of the Church
> may God give you pardon and peace,
> and I absolve you from your sins
> in the name of the Father, and of the Son
> and of the Holy Spirit.'

The penitent answers 'Amen.'

### Giving Praise to God

The priest encourages the penitent to give praise to God.

### Conclusion

The priest says, 'The Lord has freed you from your sins. Go in peace.' The penitent spends some time in prayer of thanksgiving after celebrating the sacrament.

# UNIT VI

# THE CHRISTIAN COMMUNITY — THE CHURCH

# CHRISTIAN COMMUNITIES

## CHAPTER 30 ▼

### A Christian Community, First Century A.D.

'. . . They spent their time in learning from the apostles taking part in the fellowship, and sharing in the fellowship meals and the prayers. Many miracles and wonders were being done through the apostles, and everyone was filled with awe. All the believers continued together in close fellowship and shared their belongings with one another. They would sell their property and possessions, and distribute the money among all, according to what each one needed. Day after day they met as a group in the Temple, and they had their meals together in their homes, eating with glad and humble hearts, praising God, and enjoying the good will of all the people. And every day the Lord added to their group those who were being saved . . . The group of believers was one in mind and heart. No one said that any of his belongings was his own, but they all shared with one another everything they had. With great power the apostles gave witness to the resurrection of the Lord Jesus, and God poured rich blessings on them all. There was no one in the group who was in need. Those who owned fields or houses would sell them, bring the money received from the sale, and hand it over to the apostles; and the money was distributed to each one according to his need.'
(Acts 2:42–47; Acts 4:32–35)

## An Early Irish Monastery, Sixth and Seventh Century A.D.

In early Christian Ireland, some people were called by God to live together in special communities. Each community lived in a monastery or *monastic settlement*.

In lonely places such as the mountains of Glendalough or Sceilig Rock Island, the monks lived together in poverty, obeying the Abbot (who was in charge of the community) and helping one another to love God and each other.

The community lived in small houses hardly better than huts. The church was the most important building. There was also a refectory (dining room), a kitchen, a pool or washing place and a guest-house. These buildings were all enclosed by a ditch.

Work began early in the morning after prayer and readings from Scripture. Some monks worked in the fields, ploughing, sowing and reaping. Others worked as teachers, scholars or artists. Still more worked in the flour mill or at the kiln making dishes. The cook and the baker were kept busy, as were the carpenter and the blacksmith. Everyone took turns to serve in the refectory. The food consisted mainly of bread, vegetables and fish. Wednesday and Friday were always 'fast' days, when the monks ate even less bread than usual. In fact the Irish for Wednesday, 'An Chéadaoin', means, 'the first fast'. Thursday, 'An Déardaoin' means 'between the fasts'; Friday, 'An Aoine', means 'the fast'.

The monks spent much of their time praying together in the church, praying alone in their huts or 'cells', and reading the Scriptures. They even got up during the night to pray. Mass was celebrated on Sundays and feast days. St Colm Cille in his advice to monks declared that a monk 'should forgive all people from his heart and should pray constantly. He should love God above all and his neighbour as himself.'

▲
*A picture of St Luke in an early Irish manuscript*

◀ *Glendalough*

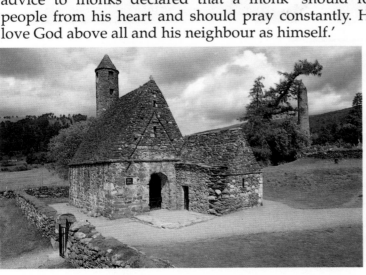

### The Corrymeela Community

The Corrymeela community is a group of Christians in Ireland who believe that God has called them together to be peacemakers. The aim of the community is to work for a society in which every person is respected, and in which the wealth is shared by all the people, so that there will be real peace. Some members of the Corrymeela community live at Ballycastle, County Antrim. Many people come to this reconciliation centre to rest, to think and to build up their relationship with others. The families of prisoners; people whose relations were killed in the violence in the North; single parents; school groups; unemployed young people; youth clubs; senior citizens; and handicapped groups — all are welcomed. Jesus calls every Christian to be a peacemaker. The Corrymeela community is answering that call by working to end violence and set up a society of peace and well-being for everyone.

*A group of young people enjoying themselves at a Corrymeela reconciliation centre* ▶

# QUESTIONS

1. List all the things which the people in the first example did because they were part of the Christian community.
2. How did being in a community help an early Irish monk to be a better Christian?
3. What effects do the members of the Corrymeela community have on the people they meet?
4. Are there any similarities between these three different Christian communities?
5. What are the differences between them?

Since the time of the very first Christians, the followers of Jesus have lived in communities. There are many different kinds of Christian community. A school, a family, a prayer group, the St Vincent de Paul Society, the employees in a factory, a football team or a class can all be Christian communities. Every Christian needs the community to help him or her to follow God's plan. The community needs every Christian to help to keep it united, strong and loving. Another name for the Christian community is the 'Church'. Each small community is part of a Parish and every Parish is part of a Diocese. All the Diocesan communities together make up the world Church. We use the word 'catholic' to describe the Church because it means 'worldwide'.

# EXERCISES

1.  List the Christian communities (large and small) to which you belong.
2.  Pick three of these communities and explain how each of them gives you opportunities to be a better Christian.
3.  How could you help to improve each of these communities?
4.  Make a diagram or poster to show your place in the World Church Community (include your parish and diocese).
5.  Why do you think that the building in which the Christian community prays and celebrates the sacraments is called 'a church'?

◀ *Pope John Paul II*

*Reflection*: 'So we are to use our different gifts in accordance with the grace that God has given us. If our gift is to preach God's message, we must do it . . . If it is to serve, we must serve; if it is to teach, we must teach. If it is to encourage others, we must do so . . .

Work hard and do not be lazy . . . Let your hope keep you joyful, be patient in your troubles, and pray at all times. Share your belongings with your needy brothers and open your homes to strangers.' Romans 12:6–8, 11–13

*Action*: Join a group or organisation in your local Church community which tries to help others. If there is no suitable organisation, ask your teacher or some other adult to help you set one up.

*Song*: 'One Bread, One Body'

*Prayer*: Lord, thank you for the gift of the Church community. May we always be willing to play our part in the life of that community. Amen.

# THE CHRISTIAN COMMUNITY IN MY PARISH

## CHAPTER 31
▼

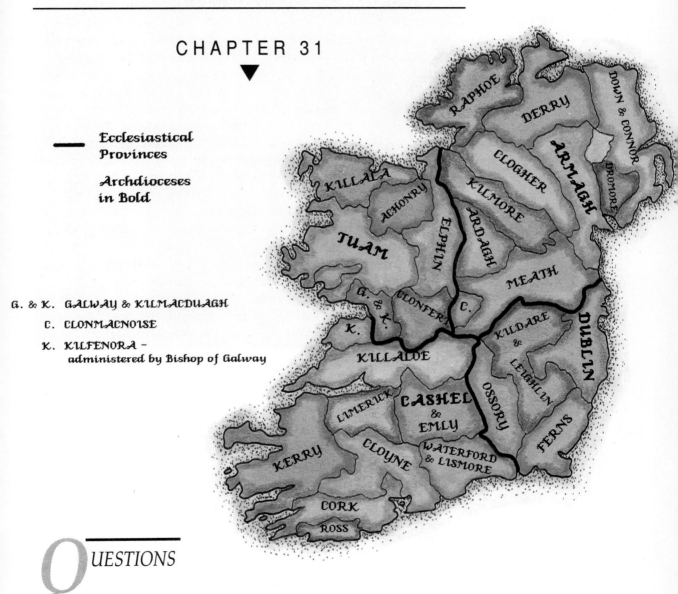

— Ecclesiastical
Provinces

Archdioceses
in Bold

G. & K. GALWAY & KILMACDUAGH

C. CLONMACNOISE

K. KILFENORA –
administered by Bishop of Galway

## QUESTIONS

1.  Can you find your diocese on this map?
2.  Can you find the general area of your parish on this map?

In every country in the world the Church is divided into *dioceses*. The Bishop in each area is responsible for the people in his diocese. Each diocese is divided into *parishes*.

When you see people in your community trying to live out Christ's commandment to 'love one another', then you see your parish in action. It is part of God's plan that the people in the Church will help the community in different ways.

'There are different kinds of spiritual gifts, but the same Spirit gives them. There are different ways of serving, but the same Lord is served . . . God gives ability to everyone for their service. The Spirit's presence is shown in some way in each one, for the good of all . . . In the Church, God has put all in place . . . Apostles . . . prophets . . . teachers . . . those who perform miracles . . . those who are given the power to heal or help others, or to direct them . . .' (1 Corinthians 12:4–7, 28)

In the Church community today, parents have the responsibility of educating their children in the faith and giving them a loving example. The energy and enthusiasm of young people helps to keep the Church community vibrant. Their imagination and readiness to help benefits everyone.

The priest has the task of representing Jesus in the celebration of the sacraments. The bishop teaches the Christians in his diocese about Jesus' message. The Pope, who is called 'the Servant of the Servants of God', helps the world Church community to be strongly united.

# QUESTIONS

1. According to the biblical passage, why does God give us gifts?
2. What tasks do the following people have in the Church community: parents; postmen/women; doctors; bricklayers; journalists?
3. Who is the bishop of your diocese?

In our parish community celebrations, each of us may have very different work to do, but it is all equally important. If every person in the community does not help to make the celebration of the sacraments as rich as possible, then it is like a cake with some of the ingredients missing or a football team without a goalie; it is not as good as it could be, there is something vital missing. Some important jobs connected with the community celebrations include:

*Sacristan:* is in charge of keeping the whole church ready for the celebration of the sacraments.

*Ministers of the Eucharist:* assist the priest to distribute Holy Communion to the people who are present at the celebration of the Eucharist and to those confined to home. For example: the sick, the handicapped.

*Ministers of the Word:* read passages from Scripture at Mass.

*Altar Servers:* assist the priest during the celebration of the sacraments.

*Church collectors:* distribute and collect baskets which are passed around at Mass to collect money for the upkeep of the churches in the dioceses.

*Church cleaners:* keep the church building in good condition.

*Members of the Altar Committee:* decorate the altar and keep the altar cloths clean and ironed.

*Ushers:* welcome people to the church and show them to their seats.

*Musicians:* provide music and/or singing to help the community 'raise their hearts and minds to God'.


# EXERCISES

1. What is the name of your parish?
2. Find out how many people there are in your parish.
3. Who is the parish priest and who are the curates?
4. Mention three activities that take place in your parish which show a community working together. Give a detailed account of at least one.

*Reflection*: 'Love one another warmly as Christian brothers, and be eager to show respect for one another. Work hard and do not be lazy. Serve the Lord with a heart full of devotion. Let your hope keep you joyful, be patient in your troubles, and pray at all times. Share your belongings with your needy fellow-Christians, and open your homes to strangers.' Romans 12:10–13

*Action*: Pay a visit to the sacristan of your local church. Offer to help with the work of keeping the church nice, for example, keeping the grounds tidy; keeping the inside of the church clean and tidy; keeping the bookstall neat and tidy.

*Song*: 'Walk in the Light'

*Prayer*: Lord, thank you for my parish. Help me to appreciate the work that is done by all the different people to make it a good place in which to live and worship God. Amen.

# THE CHRISTIAN COMMUNITY IN MY LIFE

## CHAPTER 32

The Trial of the Scillitan Christians, North Africa, A.D. 180

| | |
|---|---|
| *Narrator:* | On the seventeenth day of July, at Carthage, there were brought before the court: Speratus, Nartzalus, Cittinus, Donata, Secunda, Vestia and others. Saturninus the Proconsul conducted the trial. |
| *Saturninus the Proconsul:* | By the mercy of the Emperor you can go free from this court, if you return to your senses. |
| *Speratus:* | We have never done any wrong, we have not committed any crime, we have never spoken ill, in fact, even when punished for nothing we have given thanks. That is because we are loyal to the Emperor — our Emperor. |
| *Saturninus:* | I don't see what the problem is. We are very tolerant to religious people. We too are very religious. Our religion is simple. All we want you to do is to swear by the greatness of our lord the Emperor and pray for his welfare. We do it; you ought to do so too. |
| *Speratus:* | If you will just listen, I'll explain to you the mysteries of our belief; they too are simple. |
| *Saturninus:* | I will not listen if you intend to speak evil against our traditions. All I want to hear is an oath from you in the name of the Emperor of the Roman World. |
| *Speratus:* | The empire of this world I know not; but rather I serve that God whom no man hath seen nor with these eyes can see; I have committed no theft; in fact if I buy anything I pay the tax. I am a responsible citizen because I know my Lord, the King of Kings and the Emperor of all nations. |

| | |
|---|---|
| *Saturninus to the rest of the accused:* | At least the rest of you don't be obstinate. Cease to be of this criminal persuasion. |
| *Speratus:* | Are you persuading us to break the law of the land by telling a lie? |
| *Saturninus:* | I'm asking you to stop this foolishness for your own sakes. |
| *Cittinus:* | We have nothing to fear, except letting down our Lord God who is in heaven. |
| *Donata:* | Honour belongs to Caesar as Caesar, but our first loyalty is to God. |
| *Vestia:* | I am a Christian too. |
| *Secunda:* | I am a Christian and I don't want to be anything else. |
| *Saturninus to Speratus:* | Do you persist in being a Christian? |
| *Speratus:* | I am a Christian. |
| *Narrator:* | And with him they all agreed. |
| *Saturninus:* | Do you want some time to think about it? |
| *Speratus:* | There's nothing to think about; it's so straight-forward that there's no need. |
| *Saturninus:* | What are the things in that box you have with you? |
| *Speratus:* | Just some books. |
| *Saturninus:* | Are they magic spells? |
| *Speratus:* | No, they are just copies of letters from Paul, a just man. |
| *Saturninus:* | I'll give you one last chance; have a delay of thirty days to think it out. |
| *Speratus:* | I've told you; I'm a Christian. There will be no changing of my mind. |
| *Narrator:* | And with him they all agreed. |
| *Narrator:* | Saturninus the Proconsul read out the decree from the tablet concerning Speratus, Nartzalus, Cittinus, Donata, Vestia, Secunda and the rest. Having confessed that they lived according to the Christian way, and after being offered the opportunity of returning to the custom of the Romans, having continued to persist obstinately in their belief, it is determined that they be put to the sword. |

| | |
|---|---|
| *Speratus:* | We give thanks to God. |
| *Nartzalus:* | Today we are martyrs in heaven; thanks be to God. |
| *Narrator:* | Saturninus the Proconsul ordered it to be declared to the herald: Speratus, Nartzalus, Cittinus, Verturius, Felix, Aquilinas, Laetantius, Januaria, Generosa, Vestia, Donata and Secunda, I have ordered to be executed. |
| *Narrator:* | Those sentenced all said: Thanks be to God. |

taken from Janet Green, *Harlequinade*, Transcript of the trial

Being a Christian has never been easy. However, most Christians today are not asked to die for their faith even though there have been martyrs in our own day. For the Christians of Carthage in North Africa, nearly two thousand years ago, their faith was so important that they were willing to be 'put to the sword' rather than reject their God.

# QUESTIONS

1. What did Saturninus the Proconsul (a Roman official) want the Christians to do?
2. Why were the Christians unwilling to do what he asked?
3. In your opinion were the Christians just being stubborn and stupid or brave followers of Jesus?

Although most of us will not be asked to die for our faith, living in the Christian community takes a lot of courage, strength of character and energy. There will always be people ready to laugh or jeer at us when we try to do the right thing. The student who continues with his/her work while everyone else wastes time; the teenager who refuses to take drugs even though 'everyone is doing it'; the young person who gets up early every morning during Lent to take part in the Eucharist although none of his/her friends go: these are all examples of people trying to follow God's way in caring for their mind, their body and their relationship with God.

# EXERCISES

1. What gifts do you have to offer to the Christian community?
2. What do you find most difficult about being a Christian
   (a) at home
   (b) at school
   (c) as a member of the Church community
   (d) in your social life?
3. What would your answer have been to Saturninus the Proconsul if he had asked you if you wanted thirty days to think out whether or not you wanted to be a Christian?
4. Do a short study of a Christian who suffered or died for his or her faith (for example Maximilian Kolbe, St Stephen, St Agnes, Archbishop Romero). Present your findings to the class, or display them in the classroom.

*Reflection*: 'But other people are like the seeds sown in good soil. They hear the message, accept it, and bear fruit; some thirty, some sixty, and some a hundred.' Mark 4:20

*Action*: Keep a look-out during the coming week for opportunities to stand up for your faith. Notice what circumstances discourage you from being a 'brave' Christian.

*Song*: 'Blest be the Lord'

*Prayer*: Lord, may we always appreciate the gift of faith which you have given us through the Christian community. Help us to use every opportunity to really live that faith. Amen.

# ECUMENISM

▼

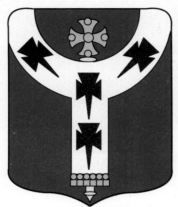

## CHAPTER 33

*St Peter's Cross, used by the
Roman Catholic Church*

*The Canterbury Cross, used by
the Anglican Church*

*The Cross of St Athanasius,
used by the Greek Orthodox
Church*

*An emblem used by the World
Council of Churches*

*A cross used by the
Russian Orthodox
Church*

## QUESTIONS

1. Do you recognise any of these emblems?
2. Do they have anything in common?
3. Do you know of any similar emblems?
4. What do they represent?

The emblem of the ship on the previous page is used by the World Council of Churches. The other four emblems are each used by a different Christian denomination. All of the emblems include the sign of the cross. This shows that each of the Churches believes in Jesus and his message of love. In spite of this, the Churches are separated from each other because they do not agree on all matters to do with their faith.

The World Council of Churches is an organisation, set up in 1948, which meets in different parts of the world every six or seven years. They meet to worship together, to discuss important questions of faith and to work towards unity. Not all Christians are members of this group but its work is of interest to all. Ecumenism is the name given to the efforts that Christians are making to understand and respect each other and grow towards ultimate unity in Christ.

# QUESTIONS

1. List as many different Christian Churches as you can.
2. How many of these have members in your local area?
3. Do you know anyone from another Christian Church?
4. What do you know of the beliefs or ways of worship of any other Christian Church?
5. Have you ever talked to them about their faith? Why? Why not?

The first major division within Christianity happened more than 1,000 years after the birth of Jesus. The western and eastern parts of the Church had been drifting apart for several centuries. The people in the West used Latin and those in the East used Greek. Arguments about how the East and West would be ruled and disagreements about some religious ideas led to the final split in A.D.1054. The eastern half of the Church is known as the 'Eastern Orthodox Church'. In Russia this is called the 'Russian Orthodox Church', in Greece it is the 'Greek Orthodox Church', and so on in individual countries.

The second major division is called the 'Reformation'. It began in Germany in the sixteenth century. A monk called Martin Luther spoke publicly about his dissatisfaction with the way people were living their Christian lives. He believed that they were not paying enough attention to reading and living the Scriptures and were too superstitious. Martin Luther wanted to bring the Catholic Church back to the way he thought it should be. The Roman Catholic Church leaders knew that some changes were necessary but did not agree with all of Luther's demands. In 1521 Luther was excommunicated (this means he was no longer a member of the Roman Catholic Church). Luther's supporters became known as 'Protestants'.

Other people such as John Calvin followed Luther's example. Over the years, further efforts were made to improve the Protestant Church and this led to further divisions. In England, the Anglicans were formed in 1536 when the English parliament declared that Henry VIII, and not the Pope, was the head of the Church of England. In the eighteenth century, John Wesley tried to improve the Anglican Church and his followers became known as Methodists.

▲
*Martin Luther*

# *Q*UESTION

1. Why do you think the divisions among the Churches have caused bitterness and even wars over the centuries?

# *E*XERCISE

1. Find out some more information on the Reformation or on the split between the Eastern and Western Churches. Share your findings with the rest of your class.

In the Scriptures Jesus prayed that his disciples would be united so that the world would believe in him. 'I pray that they may all be one. Father! . . . May they be one, so that the world will believe that you sent me.' (John 17:21). If all Christians could work together as one community to spread the Gospel, they would be better witnesses to Jesus. As Christians we all have a duty to get to know and understand those Christians who are separated from us by differences of belief or practice. The ecumenical movement has had some success, particularly in encouraging goodwill among Christians, but the task is not easy.

# ASSIGNMENT

Divide into groups of five or six and each group choose one of the following religious groups: Church of Ireland; Presbyterian Church; Methodist Church; Quakers; Greek Orthodox. Do a project on your chosen religion, making sure to include the following information:

1. When was it founded and by whom?
2. What are its main beliefs?
3. What beliefs does it share with the Roman Catholic Church?
4. In what ways is it different from the Roman Catholic Church?
5. How many people of that religion are there in Ireland today?
6. If possible, invite a member of your chosen religious group to come and talk to your class and answer questions.

*Reflection*: 'John spoke up: "Master, we saw a man driving out demons in your name, and we told him to stop, because he doesn't belong to our group." "Do not try to stop him," Jesus said to him and to the other disciples, "Because whoever is not against you is for you."' Luke 9:49–50

*Action*: Organise a prayer service with some young Christians of different Churches in your school or area. (Chapter 43 may be of help to you.) Perhaps you could plan to have some refreshments and music afterwards.

*Song*: 'We Are One in the Spirit'

*Prayer*: Lord, bless all Christians. By growing closer to you may we grow closer to each other. Amen.

# UNIT VII

# THE LITURGICAL YEAR

# MISSION

## CHAPTER 34

**Instructions**

This is a game for four people. One is the jailer, three are rescuers.

*The Jailer*

1.  The jailer has to keep the prisoners in the jail, or recapture them if they are rescued.
2.  The jailer has two guards.
3.  The jailer must throw the dice in turn in order to move the guards in 'No Man's Land'.
4.  The jailer may not move the guards into 'Free Country'.
5.  The jailer may only enter or leave the jail by the blue squares.

*The Rescuers*

1.  The rescuers have to rescue the prisoners from the jail and get them back safely to 'Free Country', through 'No Man's Land'.
2.  Each rescuer has one rescuer counter to start with. The rescuer may move freely in 'Free Country' (without throwing the dice) when it is his/her turn.

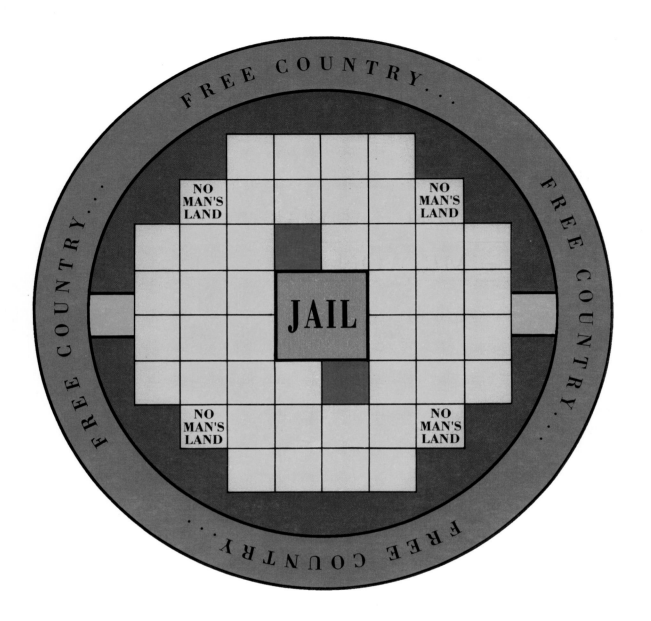

3. Each rescuer must throw the dice in turn to move his/her counter in 'No Man's Land'.
4. The rescuers may only enter or leave the jail by the blue squares.
5. The rescuers may only enter or leave 'Free Country' by the green squares.
6. Once a prisoner counter is brought to 'Free Country', it becomes a rescuer counter, and may be used by the player who rescued it to rescue more prisoners.

### How to Rescue Prisoners

1. Following the score on the dice, a counter lands on a prisoner counter in jail.
2. The rescuer moves them both together back to 'Free Country' following the score on the dice.

### How to Capture Prisoners

1. The jailer may capture a rescuer, or a rescuer and prisoner together, by landing a guard on top of them following the score on the dice.
2. The jailer moves the prisoner or prisoners directly back to the jail, without throwing the dice.
3. Any rescuer counter captured in this way becomes a prisoner, and must wait to be rescued.
4. If a guard lands on a rescuer in jail, the rescuer automatically becomes a prisoner and must wait to be rescued.
5. Rescuers and prisoners may be captured in the blue or green squares.

### The Winner

1. The jailer wins if there are six or fewer rescuer counters at the end of the game
2. The rescuers win if there are seven or more rescuer counters at the end of the game.

### To Start

1. You will need:
   (a) Two counters of the same colour for guard counters
   (b) A number of different colour counters for prisoner and rescuer counters. For example: four yellow, four red, and four green counters — one colour for each rescuer.
2. The jailer places the guard counters in jail.
3. Each rescuer places a rescuer counter in 'Free Country'.
4. All the other counters are prisoners, and the jailer puts them in jail.
5. The rescuers take their turns first, one at a time.
6. The jailer throws last.
7. It is best to set a time limit, for example one class period.

A mission is a special task, usually done to help others in some way, and which is often difficult or dangerous. Some missions can be attempted by individuals, while others are best attempted by a team of people. In the game at the beginning of this chapter, the rescuers must cooperate in order to rescue as many prisoners as possible. A space mission to find out more about the universe would be impossible without teamwork. Missions can be exciting, but they also need a lot of hard work and preparation which can be quite boring.

# EXERCISES

1. Do you know of any famous missions? Describe one to the class.
2. In what kind of mission would you like to take part? Explain.

The Christian community has a special mission and all of us are part of the mission team. Our task is to show God's love to everyone in the world and to tell them the Good News of the Gospel, the message of Jesus. Whether people are poor, rich, far away, next door, happy, lonely, afraid, young, old, enemy or friend, our mission is to care about their needs, respect them and serve them in any way we can. Helping rich people to understand that they must share their wealth in order to be happy is just as important as helping to provide jobs for unemployed people. Encouraging each other in the Christian community to pray more and really take part fully in the sacraments is important to our mission since Christians also need to be reminded that God loves them. Young people have a special mission to help each other to build a strong community by being loving rather than selfish. Young people are called to help spread this love, especially to the downtrodden, the neglected, those who are near to home and those far away. They can do this by getting involved in any activities to help others and praising one another for the efforts that each one is making. The Christian mission is difficult at times and can be dangerous in some parts of the world. But it can also be joyful and exciting. For example, when 'missionaries' in inner city Dublin see a woman who used to live rough, now enjoying the peace and security of her own home, they are thrilled. They have brought God's message of hope and love to the woman and helped her to return to the community.

# ASSIGNMENT

Divide into groups of four or five. Each group chooses a different part of the Christian mission and prepares a project presentation about it for the rest of the class. (You might choose a place like India, Tanzania or your local area; or you could choose a group, for example the elderly, travellers, politicians or teenagers; or you could choose certain well-known missionaries such as Mother Theresa, the White Fathers or Concern.) Your project should include

(a) the special needs of the area or group or person
(b) in what ways God's love is being brought to people to help or to challenge them
(c) bringing to people the Good News of Jesus.

*Reflection*: 'Suppose there are brothers or sisters who need clothes and don't have enough to eat. What good is there in your saying to them, God bless you! Keep warm and eat well! if you don't give them the necessities of life? So it is with faith; if it is alone and has no actions with it, then it is dead.' James 2:15–17

*Action*: Decide as a class on some 'action for mission' which you can perform throughout the coming year. (Remember, although fund-raising is important, there are other equally important things in the mission of the community. For example, helping people to get to know Jesus.)

*Song*: 'Here I Am, Lord'

*Prayer*: Lord, on Mission Sunday we celebrate the fact that your love reaches out to others through us. Thank you for this great gift. Amen.

# ALL SOULS AND
# ALL SAINTS

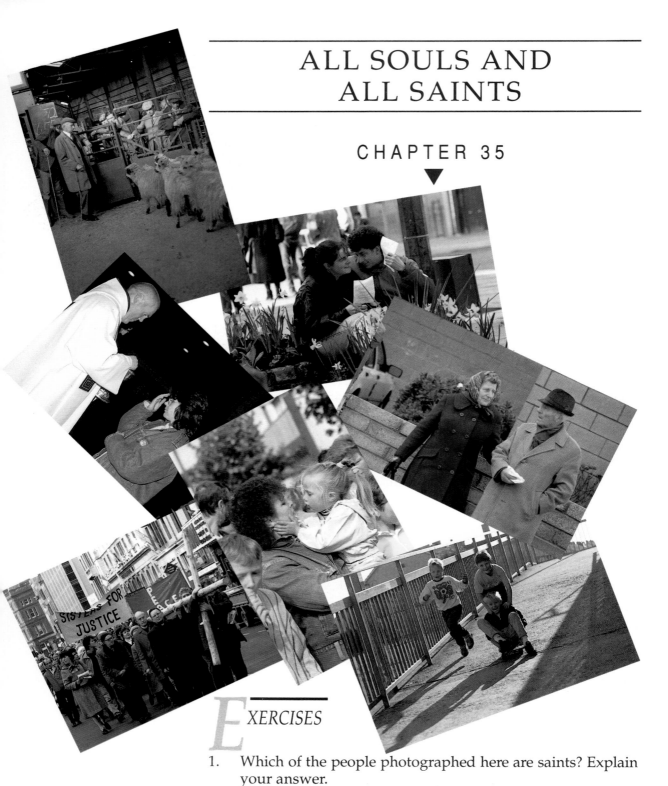

## CHAPTER 35

## EXERCISES

1. Which of the people photographed here are saints? Explain your answer.
2. Does your photograph belong here? Why/why not?

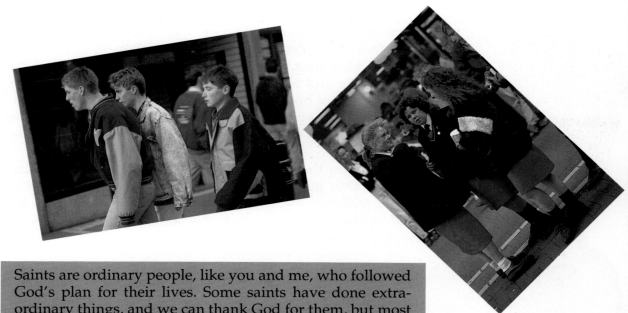

Saints are ordinary people, like you and me, who followed God's plan for their lives. Some saints have done extraordinary things, and we can thank God for them, but most saints are 'ordinary'. Every year the Christian community celebrates certain 'feast' or 'holy' days. These are days when we remember the important and special things that God has done for us (Easter, or Christmas for example). We also remember Christian saints who have shown us examples of how to live as Christians. There are far too many saints for us to be able to have a separate holy day for each one. Therefore on All Saints' Day we celebrate all the saints who have lived in the Christian community, and we thank God for their example. We also ask them to pray to God for us.

# EXERCISES

1. Who is your patron saint? (Usually a saint with the same name as you. Sometimes a saint whose feast day was being celebrated on or near the day you were born. Sometimes people have a patron saint because of their work, the type of life they lead, or where they live.)

2. Prepare a short project on your patron saint. Remember to include how you could learn from this saint to be a better Christian.

3. Find out how the Christian community celebrates the important holy days. For example how will we celebrate All Saints' Day?

Some people who have died are not yet ready to meet God face to face. They need to prepare themselves to live forever with God. They may be sorry for the ways in which they have been unloving and for the times when they didn't show love. We do not know how long people spend 'in' purgatory. Perhaps they do not even notice time passing in the way that we do. However, they do have the opportunity really to examine themselves.

They can see themselves as they really are and can realise how much they need God. Each year we celebrate the Feast of All Souls and pray to God for them. We also thank God for the special opportunity which we will all have, if necessary, to prepare ourselves to meet Him face to face.

*St Patrick*

# EXERCISES

1. Compose a prayer to God for those in purgatory.
2. Those in purgatory are part of the Christian Church. How can they be an example to us?

*Reflection*: 'Our brothers, we want you to know the truth about those who have died, so that you will not be sad, as are those who have no hope. We believe that Jesus died and rose again, and so we believe that God will take back with Jesus those who have died believing in him.' 1 Thessalonians 4:13–14

*Action*: Pray for those in purgatory throughout the month of November.

*Song*: 'City of God'

*Prayer*: Lord, we thank you for the example of your saints, who have allowed your Holy Spirit to be evident in their words and actions. Help us to be saints in our turn. Amen.

*St Brigid's Cross*

## CHAPTER 36

▼

THE CONCERN FAST WILL BE ON SOON. CAN WE GET THE COLLECTION BOXES IN SCHOOL AS USUAL?

ALL THE FAMILY WILL BE HERE THIS YEAR; WE'LL HAVE GREAT FUN!

I JUST DON'T KNOW HOW WE'RE GOING TO MANAGE THIS YEAR. KIDS JUST DON'T UNDERSTAND ABOUT THE DOLE.

I REALLY LIKED THE NEW HYMNS FOR ADVENT AT THE FOLK MASS.

SO THE BIG SPENDING SEASON IS HERE AGAIN. LOTS OF FALSE "GOOD WILL" EVERYWHERE. MAYBE I CAN SLEEP THROUGH IT.

I THINK I'LL ASK FOR A RACER THIS YEAR- EVERYONE ELSE HAS ONE.

I LOVE THE ADVENT WREATH. WE HAVE ONE AT HOME AS WELL AS AT SCHOOL.

THE COLOURED LIGHTS AND DECORATIONS MAKE CHRISTMAS SEEM SO NEAR. I HOPE IT SNOWS THIS YEAR!

LET'S START COLLECTING EARLY THIS TIME FOR THE HAMPERS. THEN WE CAN GIVE THEM TO THE ST VINCENT DE PAUL IN GOOD TIME.

IT WILL SOON BE TIME TO START MAKING THE CAKES AND PUDDINGS I SUPPOSE.

## QUESTIONS

1. What kind of person might make each of these statements?
2. Could any of these statements be your thoughts during Advent?
3. How do you and your family usually prepare for Christmas?

Advent is the time when the Christian community prepares to celebrate the birth of Jesus, when God shared His son Jesus with us, so that we should share God's love with one another. The Eucharistic celebrations for the four Sundays of Advent have as their general theme 'Waiting and Hoping for the Lord'. During Advent we recall how the people of the Old Testament waited for the Messiah with hope and longing. It is easy for us to take Jesus' birth and life among us for granted, and perhaps forget that only for Jesus, we would not be certain that God loves us and will raise us from the dead on the last day. That is why it is important to use Advent as a time to think about the difference Jesus makes in our lives. It can also be a time in which to examine our lives and see if we are really sharing Jesus' love for the world as well as we can: getting the world ready for Jesus when he comes again.

# THINGS TO DO

1. One of the best ways of preparing to celebrate Jesus' birth is to welcome his brothers and sisters and especially those in need, throughout Advent. Make a list of practical ways in which your class could prepare in this way for Christmas. Choose which ones you will put into practice.
2. Design some posters to help people prepare for Christmas during Advent. The posters should encourage people to think about the real meaning of Christmas.
3. Make an Advent wreath, and plan to hold short prayer services to include the lighting of the candles during religion class each week during Advent.

*Reflection*: 'So John went throughout the whole territory of the river Jordan, preaching, "Turn away from your sins and be baptised, and God will forgive your sins . . ." The people asked him, "What are we to do, then?" He answered, "Whoever has two shirts must give one to the man who has none, and whoever has food must share it."' Luke 3:3, 10–11

*Action*: Try to help your family prepare for the coming of Jesus at Christmas. Find a way in which your family could prepare to welcome Jesus by sharing God's love at Christmas time.

*Song*: 'Our God Reigns'

*Prayer*: Lord, thank you for the opportunity we have in Advent to prepare properly for your coming. Let us not waste these few weeks. Amen.

# CHRISTMAS

▼

# QUESTIONS

1. Each of these cards has a Christmas 'sign' on it. In your opinion, which of these is the best sign for Christmas? Explain.
2. Do you think any of the signs are not good signs of Christmas? Explain.

# EXERCISE

1. Draw or describe a sign which means 'Christmas' for you.

The Christian community celebrates Christmas for many reasons. We want to thank God for loving us so much that He sent His son, Jesus, to be one of us. One way in which we celebrate this gift is to share God's love with one another, our families, our friends and other members of our community.

On the first Christmas night the angels sang:

'Glory to God in the highest heaven, and peace on earth to those with whom He is pleased.'

At Christmas we take the opportunity to be reconciled and at peace with one another, remembering that Jesus is among us, uniting us in love.

Christmas is also a time when we thank God for our own families, as we remember the little family at Bethlehem. All over the world, Christians make great efforts to be together with their families on Christmas Day.

# THINGS TO DO

1.  Make a list of the ways in which your school could become a place of peace and goodwill as you approach the Christmas season. Decide on some which your class will help put into action.
2.  Christmas is a reminder that a Christian should be joyful. Are there any Christmas customs of which you are aware, which often bring misery rather than joy at this time? How could these customs be changed so that Christmas would bring more joy to people?
3.  Find out about the ways in which Christmas is celebrated in different parts of the world.

**How Well Do You Know the Christmas Story?**

People have always loved to hear the story of the First Christmas. The Gospel writers give us just a short account of what happened, and so from the earliest times people have added details to the story. Can you remember what the Gospels tell us about the First Christmas? Try to answer the following questions:

1.  How did Mary and Joseph travel to Bethlehem?
2.  How did the inn-keeper treat them?
3.  Where in Bethlehem was Jesus born?
4.  What was the weather like on the first Christmas Day?
5.  What animals were there with the Holy Family?
6.  How many wise men came to visit Jesus in Bethlehem?
7.  How did they travel to Bethlehem?
8.  When did the wise men arrive in Bethlehem?

When you have finished, check your answers by reading Matthew 2 and Luke 2:1–20. Tell the others in your class if you find anything interesting.

*Reflection / Action / Prayer*:  Plan and celebrate a nativity play based on Matthew 1:12–18 and Luke 2:1–21.

Song:  'Ding, Dong, Merrily on High'

# LENT AND HOLY WEEK

## CHAPTER 38

An active volcano is a dangerous neighbour. After an eruption, the countryside for miles around is buried in layers of volcanic lava and ash. In spite of the danger people continue to live near such volcanoes, because the soil is so fertile. The eruption which causes such destruction enables the land to produce bumper harvests.

Lent is a time in which we prepare to celebrate Easter. Throughout the forty days from Ash Wednesday to Holy Saturday, members of the Christian community make a special effort to turn away from sin and come back to God. Lent is an opportunity for us to tackle any particular faults or failings we may have which are preventing us from being the loving people we are meant to be. It is also a time for the community to examine itself and see where it is failing in its mission to the world. During Lent we make a greater effort to be more loving, to pray more often and with better attention, and we do penance in order to become stronger Christians.

# QUESTIONS

1. How could a penance like giving up some food you really like or being kind to someone you dislike, make you a better, stronger Christian?
2. Can you explain how a volcanic eruption is a sign for Lent?

On *Ash Wednesday*, Christians take part in the *Rite of Ashes*. The priest blesses the ashes. Then he makes the sign of the cross with the ashes on each person's forehead and he might say, 'Turn away from sin and be faithful to the Gospel.'

The 'wearing' of ashes has always been a sign of repentance, or turning away from sin. When we take part in this rite at the beginning of Lent, we show that we know we are sinners, and that we will use the Lenten time to repent so that we can celebrate our new life with Jesus on Easter Sunday.

During Holy Week, the week before Easter, we celebrate the events in Jesus' life which happened during the last week of his earthly life.

*Palm (or Passion) Sunday:* We celebrate Jesus' procession into Jerusalem when the people greeted him as 'he who comes in the name of the Lord'.

*Holy Thursday:* (i) There is a morning Mass celebrated only in the Cathedral. There, the bishop blesses the oil of the sick, the oil of catechumens (those who are going to be baptised) and the chrism which will be used in the Sacraments of Baptism and Confirmation.

(ii) At the evening Mass, we celebrate the memory of the first Eucharist. At this Mass, the priest washes the feet of some of the people, because Jesus did this for his disciples at the Last Supper. At the end of this Mass, the altar is stripped and the Tabernacle left open and empty. This helps us to remember the time when Jesus was taken from us.

▲
*Jesus washes the feet of the disciples*

▲   *The Tabernacle on Holy Thursday*

*Good Friday:* We celebrate the Lord's Passion and Death in a special ceremony. The Eucharist is not celebrated on this day or on Holy Saturday. The Good Friday ceremony includes readings from the Scriptures, 'Veneration' or honouring of the cross, and a holy communion service.

▲
*Good Friday*

*Holy Saturday:* On this day the Christian community 'waits at the Lord's tomb', thinking about his suffering and death. We remember the apostles, who thought that the end had come because Jesus was dead and buried.

*Reflection*: 'Jesus knew that the Father had given him complete power; he knew that he had come from God and was going to God. So he rose from the table, took off his outer garment, and tied a towel round his waist. Then he poured some water into a basin and began to wash the disciples' feet and dry them with the towel round his waist . . . After Jesus had washed their feet, he put his outer garment back on and returned to his place at the table. "Do you understand what I have just done to you?" he asked. ". . . I have set an example for you, so that you will do just what I have done for you."' John 13:3–5, 12, 15

*Action*: Take part in all the Lenten and Holy Week celebrations as attentively as you can. Every day ask the help of the Holy Spirit in doing whatever penance you have decided on for Lent.

*Song*: 'The Lord Hears the Cry of the Poor'

*Prayer*: Lord, you have told us that we must die to selfishness if we want to rise with you in a new life of love. Give us the courage, Lord, to make this possible.  Amen.

# EASTER

CHAPTER 39

. . . the seed,
Un-dead, it is sterile,
a stone.
But dying, it brings
Life
and the August fields are golden now
with the harvest of its fertile surrender.

from *Reflections* by Hugh Lavery

The celebration of Easter begins with the *Easter Vigil*. This takes place after dark on Saturday and before dawn on Sunday. It is the moment when the Christian community is at its most happy and joyful. Jesus has risen from the dead, he has defeated death. For the followers of Jesus, death is no longer the end of everything, but the beginning of a new life.

# EXERCISE

1. The following signs are often used at Easter. Can you explain why they are good signs of Easter and of the Resurrection?

   (a) A lighted candle      (c) Newborn chicks
   (b) Eggs      (d) Lambs

*The Easter Vigil* ▶

The Easter Vigil begins with the *Service of Light*. A bonfire is lit outside the church, and the Paschal or Easter Candle is lit from it. The lighted candle is brought into the dark church as a sign that the Risen Lord Jesus is lighting up our lives. Readings from Scripture follow. These readings recall for us all the great things which God has done for us since the Creation of the world. Following this, people are often baptised into the Christian community. Even if there is no one to be baptised, everyone in the Church renews his or her *baptismal promises*. A joyful celebration of the Eucharist ends the Vigil. For the next fifty days the whole Christian community celebrates with great joy. Then on *Pentecost Sunday* the Easter season ends with the feast of the Holy Spirit. On this day we celebrate the descent of the Holy Spirit on the apostles and the presence of the Spirit in the Church today.

◀

The Resurrection of
Christ *by Murillo,
1617–82*

# E*XERCISE*

1.  Prepare a project on Easter or Resurrection or New Life.
    Cover a wall of your classroom with the projects and leave
    them up after Easter to remind you of the Easter celebration.

*Reflection*: 'God has raised this very Jesus from the dead, and
we are all witnesses to this fact.' Acts 2:32

*Action*: Decide to bring the happiness of Easter to a lonely
person this Easter Sunday. Visit them, and perhaps bring flowers or fruit.

*Song*: 'Alleluia, Alleluia, Give Thanks to the Risen Lord'

*Prayer*: Lord Jesus, we have died with you in Baptism. May we
also rise with you to new life. Alleluia.

# UNIT VIII

# WORSHIP AND PRAYER

## PRAYER

### CHAPTER 40

Brother and sister Ian and Helen Kelly lived together in their old family home. Their parents were long dead. Many years ago Ian decided that they should sell the field at the back of the house and buy a car between them. Helen thought that this was a stupid idea, and was not slow in saying so. She said that she had got by for years with her bicycle and had no need for a car. 'And you don't need a car either,' she told Ian. 'You just want to show off in front of the neighbours.' Ian was bitterly disappointed and very angry. He could not afford to buy a car on his own, and he really wanted one.

From that day on Ian refused to speak to his sister. After some weeks of being ignored, Helen apologised to Ian and said she would change her mind if having a car was so important to him. Ian would hardly listen to her. 'You can keep your worthless apology. I don't want it,' he said, and left the room, slamming the door. Now Helen was really angry, and she declared that it would be a long time before she'd speak to him again.

It was indeed a long time. Neither of them spoke a word to each other for five years. Although they continued to live in the same house, sharing the same sitting-room and kitchen, they both stubbornly behaved as if they were living alone. Some of the neighbours tried to bring about a reconciliation. The parish priest made a great effort, but it was no good. The silence continued.

One day Helen had a serious accident at work. She was rushed to hospital, where she remained for several months. Finally, Ian went to see her. The accident had shaken him and he wanted to be reconciled with his sister. Helen also had had a shock, and was glad to be friends again. They both looked forward to the time when she could go home.

Helen was delighted with the way Ian had kept the house while she was away. However, after she had told him how great everything was, and he had told her how well she was looking, there didn't seem to be much more to say. Throughout that evening, and the evenings that followed, the two of them tried to make conversation, but it was very difficult. They each found it embarrassing trying to chat pleasantly with each other. Neither of them really knew what to say, since they had lived such separate lives for so long. They found that they were strangers to each other. It took them many months before they felt relaxed and happy with each other. At one stage Helen told her friends that it would almost have been easier if there had been no reconciliation!

Later she was glad that she hadn't given up, for after a time she found that her brother had become a real friend again, someone she could rely on. The Kellys got on well together from then on, and rarely thought about the unhappy past.

# QUESTIONS

1. Why do you think the row between Ian and Helen lasted so long?
2. Why did the two Kellys find it so difficult to talk to each other after the reconciliation?

If we don't talk to our friends and listen to them, our friendship can die. The best way to keep a friendship strong is to keep in touch regularly.

# QUESTIONS

1. How do you keep in touch with your friends?
2. Have you ever lost friends by not keeping in contact with them? Explain.

Our friendship with God is similar in many ways to our other friendships. God never goes away, of course, nor does He forget about us, but *we* can ignore God at times, and act as if He wasn't there. Prayer is a very important part of keeping in touch with God. To pray means:

    (a) To allow ourselves to notice that God is with us

    (b) to talk to God, and

    (c) to listen to God's word.

Praying with others as we celebrate the sacraments, joining in prayer services and praying privately to God every day are all good ways of helping our friendship with God to grow strong. If we get into the habit of not praying, perhaps because we are 'too busy' or 'too tired' or because 'it doesn't matter this once', then our friendship with God can be weakened.

Use the following questionnaire to examine how you pray. Please consider, then answer the following questions in your copy.

1. I like to pray
   (a) in the morning
   (b) at night
   (c) in a church
   (d) by myself
   (e) with others?

2. I pray because
   (a) I know I should
   (b) it helps me
   (c) I enjoy it?

3. When I pray I
   (a) kneel
   (b) sit
   (c) stand
   (d) walk?

4. I pray using
   (a) set (formal) prayers
   (b) any thoughts that come into my head
   (c) readings from the Scriptures
   (d) music
   (e) hymns?

5. When I pray, I
   (a) pray for myself
   (b) pray for others
   (c) pray to get things
   (d) pray for help and guidance
   (e) pray to thank God?

6. I pray
   (a) often
   (b) never
   (c) sometimes?

7. I think God answers my prayers
   (a) always
   (b) sometimes
   (c) never?

▲
*Prayer group at Taizé*

# E XERCISES

1. Is your way of praying helping your friendship with God to grow strong?
2. How could you improve your prayer?

*Reflection*: 'Ask, and you will receive; seek, and you will find; knock, and the door will be opened to you. For everyone who asks will receive, and anyone who seeks will find, and the door will be opened to him who knocks. Would any of you who are fathers give your son a stone when he asks for bread? Or would you give him a snake when he asks for a fish? Bad as you are, you know how to give good things to your children. How much, then, will your father in heaven give good things to those who ask Him!' Matthew 7:7–11

*Action*: Spend a few moments before you begin talking to God, just remembering that God is with you, a loving listener, and ask the Holy Spirit of God to help you to pray.

*Song*: 'Fill Me With Your Praise'

*Prayer*: Father, we thank you for being there, always loving, never too busy to listen. Help us to grow closer to you in prayer. Amen.

# MARY

## CHAPTER 41

Do a report on Mary, wife of Joseph the carpenter, for a magazine article. Find out the following details:

| | |
|---|---|
| Full name: | |
| Age: | |
| Height: | |
| Colour of eyes: | |
| Colour of hair: | |
| State of health: | |
| Home town: | |
| Country: | |
| Religion: | |
| Marital status: | |
| Children: | |
| Employment: | |
| Qualifications: | |
| Titles: | |
| Wealth: | |
| Property: | |
| Travel: | |

## QUESTIONS

1. Where did you find most of your information?
2. List the passages in the New Testament which you found relating to Mary.
3. Was there any information you couldn't get? Why not?
4. What else could you add to your article on Mary?

The most common title for Mary is *Our Lady*. We do not know a great deal about Mary's life, but we know enough to be certain that she is indeed 'ours', that we are important to her. Mary is part of the Christian community to which all of us as followers of Jesus belong. Everyone in that community tries as best they can to help one another to be more loving, and to grow closer to God. Mary can help the community in a special way because she is so close to God. When we pray to Our Lady, she prays for us to God and in this way she helps the whole community to have a better relationship with God.

# EXERCISES

1. Do you know any set or formal prayers to Mary? Pick the one you like best and display it on a suitably decorated poster. You might prefer to compose your own prayer and use it for the poster.
2. Mary is the mother of God, and is also a mother to us. Read the account of the Wedding Feast at Cana (John 2:1–11) and explain how in this passage Mary shows that she is a mother to Jesus' followers.
3. Read John 19:25–27.

Mary's life is an example to us of how we should live as a Christian community. By agreeing to become the mother of Jesus, Mary teaches us to follow God's plan for us. Mary went through great hardship and suffering in her life: having to become a refugee in Egypt to escape King Herod; worrying about Jesus as he went about the countryside preaching and healing, knowing that he was making too many enemies; waiting while Jesus was put on trial; suffering through his passion and death on the cross. Through all this she remained faithful to God, and strong in her love; and from her example we learn to be patient when things go wrong. From Mary we also learn to work for justice and peace. In Luke 1:46–55, Mary prays in praise of God because He has 'stretched out His mighty arm and scattered the proud with all their plans. He has brought down mighty kings from their thrones and lifted up the lowly. He has filled the hungry with good things, and sent the rich away with empty hands . . .'

# EXERCISE

1. Mary cares for everyone in the Christian community today; what do you think she is most concerned about in your parish? Write a brief account.

*Reflection*: 'Mary said, "My heart praises the Lord; my soul is glad because of God my Saviour, for He has remembered me, His lowly servant! From now on all people will call me happy, because of the great things the Mighty God has done for me."' Luke 1:46–49.

*Action*: Every day ask Mary to pray for you and for the whole Christian community.

*Song*: 'The Lourdes Magnificat'

*Prayer*: Lord, you give us your mother Mary to be our mother also. Help us to follow her example in our lives. Amen.

# VISITING THE
# HOUSE OF GOD

## CHAPTER 42

## *E*XERCISE

1. These photographs contain many objects which we see in our local church building. See how many of them you can name. Check that you are correct, using the answers on the next page.

**Answers**

1. The Altar table — this is the largest piece of furniture.
2. The Presidential chair from which the celebrant leads the liturgy.
3. The Altar cloth — a large white cloth to cover the table.
4. Lighted candles signify a special meal.
5. The Missal — this book contains all the prayers and instructions for the Mass.
6. The Corporal — a small white cloth decorated with a cross placed on the altar cloth.
7. The Tabernacle where we keep the bread that has become the body of Christ. It looks like a little cupboard but it is really a shelter for God.
8. The Lamp of God, the Sanctuary Lamp, burning all the time to show that God is here.
9. The Paschal candle, or Easter candle.
10. The Chalice or cup.
11. The Paten — a small plate used for the large host.
12. The Purificator — a small cloth or towel for cleaning the chalice.
13. Basin — this catches the water poured on the priest's hands.
14. Small cloth/towel for the priest to dry his fingers.
15. Ambo/lectern/pulpit — where readings take place.
16. The Lectionary contains all the readings for all the Masses of the year.
17. The Offertory table is where the gifts for the offertory are kept until they are brought to the altar during the offertory procession.
18. Cruets — these are the small containers that hold the wine and the water.
19. The Ciborium — this contains the small hosts which will be consecrated (changed into the body of Christ) during the Mass.

God is with us at all times and in all places. In spite of this we like to set aside special places to be used for meeting God in private and community prayer and worship. In our homes this special place might be a corner of a room, or maybe a certain chair. We might have a cross or a picture to remind us of God. Some people find that nature helps them feel closer to God. So their special place might be a forest, a cave, by a river or by the sea. The community sets up a church building which can be used for the celebration of the sacraments, prayer services and personal prayer. The church can be called the House of God firstly because it is a place which helps us to be aware of God. Secondly the Blessed Eucharist, the body of Christ is 'reserved' or kept in the tabernacle of the church, which means that Jesus is there in a special way in the church. Therefore, while we can and do pray everywhere, the atmosphere in the church, with its quietness, candles lighting, and the Blessed Sacra-ment in the tabernacle, makes it a very good place in which to pray.

# QUESTIONS

1. List any special places in which you (or other people) like to pray.
2. Do you find being in a church helps you to pray, either alone or with the community? Explain.

Since the church is a special place for meeting God, how we move and act and speak there is very important. We may disturb people who are praying privately if we shout or run or make unnecessary noise. We may distract others during a community celebration of a sacrament if we chat, turn around, arrive late or leave early. However, if we speak and act well in church, we can make it a better place in which to pray, since our behaviour helps other people to realise that the church is really a special place. This does not mean that we have to be absolutely silent. At times our prayer can be exuberant, for example, very joyful singing. We can actually pray to God through our gestures and actions, as well as our words, in the ways shown in the drawings.

*Sitting still*

*Standing still*

*Kneeling*

*Kneeling and bowing the head*

*Walking slowly and quietly*

*Genuflecting*

*Making the Sign of the Cross*

*Shaking hands at the Sign of Peace*

# THINGS TO DO

Visit your local church and see all the objects mentioned on pages 155–6. Stay to pray a while.

*Reflection*: 'How I love your Temple, Almighty God! How I want to be there! I long to be in the Lord's Temple. With my whole being I sing for joy to the living God. Even the sparrows have built a nest, and the swallows have their own home; they keep their young near your altars, Lord Almighty, my king and my God. How happy are those who live in your Temple, always singing praise to you.' Psalm 84:1–4

*Action*: Make a special effort when you are in church to be prayerful in your actions, so as to help other people to pray.

*Song*: 'The Lord is Present in His Sanctuary'

*Prayer*: Lord, may your church always be a place of prayer for us so that we can come to know you better. Amen.

# PREPARING LITURGIES AND PRAYER SERVICES

## CHAPTER 43

▼

When something good happens, we thank God. When we are sad, we ask Him for comfort and strength. When we are sorry for our sins, we ask for forgiveness and help to become more loving. We can do all this on our own, by praying privately to God, but we can also pray together as a community. A good way in which to celebrate any happening or event is to prepare and share the Eucharist together. When we need to show our sorrow and forgiveness to one another, we can celebrate the Sacrament of Reconciliation as a community. Apart from these sacraments, a 'Prayer Service' can be a good way in which to celebrate Advent, Lent, Easter, Pentecost, a feast day of Our Lady or any saint, or any important event in our life. For example we can:

(a) Recall our Baptism, and promise God again that we want to choose His way

(b) Thank God for the gift of the Holy Spirit in our lives, and pray that we will be more guided by Him

(c) Ask God for healing and comfort, especially for the sick, lonely, afraid and those whose loved ones have died

(d) Thank God for the gift of our families and ask Him to help us be more loving at home

(e) Thank God for the people who serve the community as ministers of the Eucharist, ministers of the Word, deacons, priests, bishops, and the pope, and ask Him to bless their work.

▲
*Folk group*

A prayer service, like a sacrament, can include music, songs, readings from the Scriptures, readings from suitable books, poems, mimes and plays, all of which are ways of opening our minds to God, and allowing Him into our hearts.

**Preparing to Celebrate a Sacrament or Prayer Service**

1. The first thing to decide in any celebration is the theme: the main idea or event we want to celebrate. We can ask ourselves the following questions to decide on a theme:

    (a) What special reason do we have to praise and thank God?

    (b) How do we want God to help us at this time?

2. The second thing is to discover the particular gifts which the group has and which could make the celebration better. Gifts can be used in the following ways:

    (a) Art — preparing posters or banners showing the theme or explaining the readings; doing the Mass or service leaflet

    (b) Singing/music — choosing instrumental background music, songs and psalms; playing instruments, singing; choosing suitable tapes/records

    (c) Reading — choosing and reading Scripture passages; special prayers; other readings; poems, introducing different sections of the celebration

    (d) Drama — part of a Rite of Reconciliation; at the offering of gifts; thanksgiving; for Scripture readings

    (e) Movement/mime/dancing — offering gifts; readings; prayers or songs of praise and thanks

    (f) Organising surroundings — putting altar, seats and other equipment into position; lighting; flowers; decoration of area.

3. The third thing is to decide on the place in which the celebration will take place.

    (a) The classroom — to show that God is with us at all times everywhere. A school hall can be used for larger groups.

    (b) The Church — to show that we are setting aside a special time and space to remember God and ask His help. The Church can be convenient for large groups.

    (c) The oratory — a special place, where smaller groups can celebrate.

    (d) Outdoors — in a field, wood, on a mountain, beside a lake or river. These can be good places especially for small groups to celebrate in a special way.

4. The fourth thing is to divide into groups the people who will take part in the celebration, and each group becomes responsible for preparing a part of the service or sacrament. The people who are gifted at art or music will naturally form groups. However, these groups should act as leaders

of all the people celebrating, and not simply do it all themselves. For example the music groups might choose the songs and music, but must have an opportunity to practise these with the others. Apart from the art group, musicians, readers, actors, dancers, and organisers, other groups might be needed. For example, if you are preparing a Mass you might have groups in charge of:

(a) Rite of Reconciliation
(b) Offertory
(c) Prayers of the faithful
(d) Prayers of thanksgiving
(e) Sign of Peace.

5.  The fifth thing is to decide on the length of time which the celebration will take: what time is available and what can be successfully done in that time. For example one class period will not be long enough to allow people time for individual confession of sins during a Rite of Reconciliation, so a celebration of sorrow and forgiveness without the sacrament might be better used here.

(a) One class period/double class period
(b) Some time in the morning before school
(c) At lunch time
(d) After school.

A minimum of twenty minutes is necessary for a short service. The longest celebration should take no more than an hour and a half for a very special occasion. Check the length of time which each part of the celebration will take, and cut it down if necessary.

6.  The final thing before celebrating the service or sacrament is to practise those parts which can be practised. Don't overdo it — it spoils the newness of the celebration. For example if a play has been prepared on the reading from the Old Testament, this can be practised in front of the teacher, to keep it as a surprise for the rest of the class.

**Suggestions for Celebrating the Sacraments or a Prayer Service**

1.  If you are celebrating the Eucharist or Reconciliation, look up the rites described at the end of Chapters 27 and 29, to remind yourself of the different things which must be prepared.

2.  A prayer service (with or without a priest) can take the following form:

    (a) Opening song should be sung by everyone.

    (b) Short introduction or welcome to the service, explaining the theme and any special arrangements or activities (to be composed and spoken by a student).

    (c) Rite of Reconciliation: it is good to begin any community celebration with sorrow for hurting each other and forgiveness towards those who have hurt us. We can then celebrate the rest of the service with happier hearts, bearing no grudges. The examination of conscience should take account of the theme of the service.

    (d) Prayer(s) of praise and thanksgiving to God: these can be spoken or sung, and posters could be used to show our praise and thanks more clearly.

    (e) Readings:
    (i)    from the Old Testament
    (ii)   a Psalm (usually sung)
    (iii)  from the New Testament (or some other suitable reading)
    (iv)   Gospel: there is usually a Gospel acclamation sung first.

    (f) Homily or short talk, explaining the readings and why they were chosen for the theme.

    (g) Space for quiet prayer, or a special activity or drama or film connected with the theme. Background music is useful.

    (h) Prayers of the faithful: asking God to grant us our needs, especially remembering the theme of the Mass. Include prayers for:
    (i)    the needs of the community
    (ii)   the needs of the Church
    (iii)  the world
    (iv)   leaders.

    (i) Concluding speech, thanking all those who have taken part, mentioning any special moments. Anyone in the group should feel free to join in with their own comments.

    (j) Concluding song: apart from the music mentioned, songs or instrumental music may be used during any or all of these parts of the prayer service.

3. Music:
   (a) Always include music in any celebration of the sacraments or a prayer service, since 'when we sing, we pray twice'. Be sure to choose hymns that everyone (or nearly everyone) can learn to sing. Very difficult hymns may be used as solo music, perhaps to help people give thanks after receiving the Eucharist.
   (b) When celebrating the Eucharist, the following should, where possible, be sung, because they are acclamations or shouts of joy:
      (i)   the Gloria (a hymn of praise and thanks)
      (ii)  the Gospel acclamation
      (iii) the Holy, Holy
      (iv)  the memorial acclamation (after the consecration)
      (v)   the Great Amen (at the end of the Eucharistic prayer)
   (c) Look up as many different hymn books as you can, and don't keep on using the same hymns over and over. Don't forget that background instrumental music can be very good with the Penitential Rite, or the readings, or a mime, or prayers of the faithful, or the Communion service.
4.  Readings:
   (a) When you have chosen your theme, it is a good idea to use a Biblical Concordance to help you to choose suitable readings. A Concordance is a book like a dictionary. It contains important words used in the Bible, for example, love, peace, Noah, creation. The words are listed in alphabetical order. If you are preparing a service or Eucharist with the theme of 'friendship', for example, you could look up the word 'friend' in the Concordance. The book will list all the places in the Bible where the word 'friend' is mentioned. You can look up these references in your Bible and see if any of them would be useful as readings for your celebration. For the theme of 'friendship' you could also look up other words like 'love', 'sharing' and 'forgiveness'. When celebrating the Eucharist we use readings from a special book called a *Lectionary*.
   (b) One or more of the readings could be dramatised, or mimed. A very simple way to dramatise a reading is to have different people read the 'spoken' words (those in inverted commas) and let a narrator read the rest.

164

(c) The first and second readings are introduced by the readers as follows: 'A reading from the book of . . .' (and they mention the book of the Bible from which the reading is taken). At the end of these readings, the readers say, 'This is the Word of the Lord' and the other people answer, 'Thanks be to God'.

(d) When we celebrate the Eucharist the Gospel is introduced in this way:

> *Deacon/Priest:* The Lord be with you.
> *People*: And also with you.
> *Deacon/Priest:* A reading from the Holy Gospel according to St . . . (Matthew, Mark, Luke or John).
> *People:* Glory to you, Lord.

(e) Everyone may sit for the first two readings, but it is usual to stand, as a sign of respect, for the Gospel;

(f) The responsorial psalm is sung after the Old Testament reading in the celebration of the Eucharist. This can also be done in a prayer service; however, more than one psalm can be spoken or sung during a service. The psalm is called 'responsorial' because it is sung in two parts: one person (or group of people) sings the verses. After each verse the rest of the people sing the 'response'. The responsorial psalm is a good way in which to praise and thank God for His Word to us in the Scripture readings.

5.  Penitential (Reconciliation) Rite: whether this is used as a service on its own or as part of another sacrament or service, it may take the following form:

(a) Opening hymn

(b) Opening prayer — inviting the people to repent, be sorry for their sins and change their ways

(c) Reading(s) — showing God's mercy and call to repentance

(d) Examination of conscience: may be done in many forms apart from simply calling out possible sins, for example dramatised, mimed, put to music, put on posters or banners

(e) Act of sorrow: in which we tell God and each other that we are sorry for our sins

(f) Asking for God's forgiveness: if there is no individual confession of sins, this may lead directly into a reading showing God's mercy and forgiveness

(g) Individual confession of sins in private, and absolution. Background music should be provided to help people pray at this time

(h) Prayer thanking God for His goodness and love

(i) Prayers of the faithful: asking God to help us keep to His Way of Love as individuals and as a Church community

(j) Concluding prayer

(k) Concluding hymn: other hymns and instrumental music may be included at different parts of the celebration.

6. The Offering of Gifts: this always takes place in a Eucharistic celebration, but may also be used in some prayer services. Apart from the special gifts of bread and wine, you should bring to the altar objects which are signs or symbols of things in your life for which you might want to thank God. These include a bicycle lamp, basketball, photograph of a friend, food and so on.

7. The Prayers of the Faithful: these are prayers which are said by the people of the community (the faithful). The person who leads the prayer of the faithful:

(a) Mentions what the faithful should pray for

(b) Gives them a minute or two to pray, and

(c) Invites the people to pray together out loud that God will hear all the silent prayers. For example, a prayer of the faithful for the sick:

*Leader*:     We pray for those who are sick or suffering in mind or body. (Everyone prays silently for a minute or so.)

*Leader*:     Lord, hear us.

*Everyone*:  Lord, graciously hear us.

In the prayers of the faithful, we usually pray for the whole Church community, its leaders and local needs.

8. Signs and symbols:

(a) It is good to use signs and symbols appropriately when we are celebrating as a community. Apart from obvious signs like the Cross, bread, wine, water, flowers and so on, the way we stand or sit, how we speak as we pray, how we kneel or genuflect: these are all signs of what we think we are doing. If we are polite, quietly spoken and gentle with each other, we show respect for God and for each other. We show disrespect if we are noisy, rough or giddy. This does not mean that we must be silent, or very quiet all the time. It means that our actions should suit whatever is happening at the time.

(b) It is worthwhile making a special effort with signs, especially, for example, the Sign of Peace. One way to make the Sign of Peace special is to get all the people (preferably before the celebration) to make a small token like a bookmark, or a peace card, or perhaps a Christmas card if it is a Christmas Mass or service. As the people come into the place of the celebration they put a piece of paper with their name on it into a box or bag. At some point in the Mass (maybe at the Offertory), the box is passed around and each person takes a name from it. (If you get your own name, put it back and pick another one.) Do not tell anyone whose name you have. At the Sign of Peace, write a short message of peace to the person on the card or bookmark you have prepared, and then give it to them: this can only be done if all the people in the group know each other's names. Similar exercises may be done to make other signs into special occasions in the service.

There are many books available which will provide you with full prayer services or celebrations, with all the prayers and readings included. You could use these as a help or guide in planning your own celebration, but it is not good to copy them exactly. Your prayers and efforts are what the Lord wants!